Medical and Psychiatric Issues for Counsellors

The *Professional Skills for Counsellors* series, edited by Colin Feltham, covers the practical, technical and professional skills and knowledge which trainee and practising counsellors need to improve their competence in key areas of therapeutic practice.

Medical and Psychiatric Issues for Counsellors

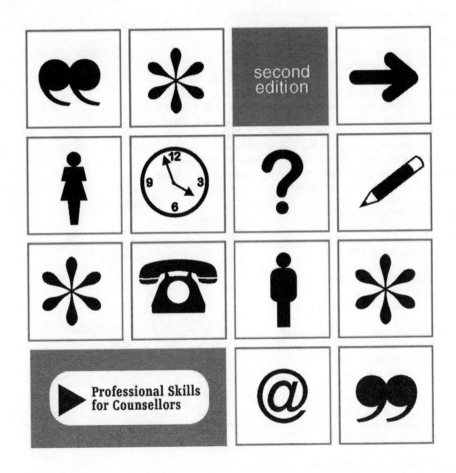

second edition

Professional Skills for Counsellors

Brian Daines
Linda Gask
and
Amanda Howe

SAGE Publications

Los Angeles • London • New Delhi • Singapore

First published 1997
Reprinted 2002, 2003, 2004
This second edition published 2007

SAGE Publications Ltd
1 Oliver's Yard
55 City Road
London EC1Y 1SP

SAGE Publications Inc.
2455 Teller Road
Thousand Oaks, California 91320

SAGE Publications India Pvt Ltd
B 1/I 1 Mohan Cooperative Industrial Area
Mathura Road
New Delhi 110 044

SAGE Publications Asia-Pacific Pte Ltd
33 Pekin Street #02-01
Far East Square
Singapore 048763

Library of Congress Control Number: 2007923071

British Library Cataloguing in Publication data

A catalogue record for this book is available from the British Library

ISBN 978-1-4129-2398-9
ISBN 978-1-4129-2399-6 (pbk)

Typeset by Cepha Imaging Pvt. Ltd., Bangalore, India
Printed and bound in Great Britain by Athenaeum Press, Gateshead
Printed on paper from sustainable resources

For Joan, John and Barry

Contents

List of figure and tables

Notes on authors

Brian Daines works primarily in independent practice. He is also Clinical Tutor in Psychosexual Medicine at the University of Sheffield and a college counsellor.

Linda Gask is Professor of Primary Care Psychiatry at the University of Manchester and an honorary Consultant Psychiatrist in Salford.

Amanda Howe is Professor of Primary Care at the Institute of Health, University of East Anglia.

Acknowledgements

There are many to whom we owe thanks for help in the writing of this book. In particular we would like to thank Tim Usherwood for his work as one of the co-authors for the first edition. We would also like specifically to mention Judith Globe from St Luke's Hospice Library in Sheffield and Ainslie Green from the University of Sheffield Counselling Service.

1

A Contextual Framework

Introduction

The first edition of this book, which was written over ten years ago, referred to the controversy, historically going back to Freud, about whether those who are not medically qualified should engage in offering psychological forms of treatment. It is an indication of the rapid period of change since then in the place of psychological therapies in treating a wide range of problems that this issue itself feels now to be a historical one. Despite this, it is still important to recognise the risks associated with counselling practice without having some working knowledge of psychiatric and medical issues and clear channels of referral through to those who can professionally evaluate psychiatric and medical symptoms where this is needed.

Despite the changes, it is still true to say that there are genuine difficulties in practising counselling outside of a medical setting and that counsellors and others still sometimes overstate the role of psychological factors in the generation of physical illness and the extent to which psychological help can be expected to be effective in certain conditions. Hopefully, as those within medicine who see all counselling as at best irrelevant and at worst dangerous have become fewer, so have the counsellors and alternative practitioners who dismiss much of medical work as ill-founded. Counsellors now generally work within a context where medical practitioners recognise the problems attached to the use of medication, especially tranquillisers, in the long-term treatment of psychological disorders. The number of short-term psychological therapies has increased and patients have become more knowledgeable about these and more willing to ask for them.

Recent Developments

The main development in the UK over the past ten years has been a change in context in the NHS within which counselling is provided. There has been a considerable extension of counselling within primary care settings so that most GPs can now refer their patients to this kind of service. Alongside this a lot of measuring and regulatory activities have arisen; regular outcome measures using CORE, NICE guidelines on evidence-based practice, clinical governance, moves towards 'stepped care' and clearer requirements in the recording of client notes. The main consequences of all this for counsellors in the NHS have been to place unfamiliar (and often unwelcome) limitations on autonomy in ways of working and an increase in administrative work.

CORE stands for Clinical Outcomes in Routine Evaluation and is a set of questionnaire forms used routinely and widely in NHS settings to evaluate risk and to provide evidence of service quality and effectiveness (CORE System Group, 1998). The NHS has also embraced the concept of clinical governance which aims 'to assure and improve clinical standards at local level throughout the NHS. This includes action to ensure risks are avoided, adverse events are rapidly detected, openly investigated and lessons learned, good practice is rapidly disseminated and systems are in place to ensure continuous improvements in clinical care' (Department of Health, 1997). Systems of clinical governance have been developed to address both quality issues in health care and public concerns about poor performance by professionals (Carter, BACP Information Sheet DG9). A key part of this is measuring performance against pre-defined standards. The basic standards for mental health care are set out in the National Service Framework (Department of Health, 2002, 2005) and more specifically in the suite of NICE guidelines published by the National Institute for Health and Clinical Excellence.

Important new areas of counselling have also emerged, for example bibliotherapy and e-therapy. Bibliotherapy is the use of books to treat mild mental health problems. These may be specifically on mental health or, for example, novels with appropriate themes. An example of bibliotherapy is the service provided by East Ayrshire Libraries in partnership with the NHS. An appointment is made with the bibliotherapist to meet for a discussion and the recommendation of appropriate books, usually with one or two follow-up sessions. E-therapy takes the form of e-mail correspondence with a counsellor or psychotherapist. It may be suitable for those who are reticent about face-to-face contact with a counsellor and those who do not live near a practice, or have restricted mobility. The usual assessments of medical and psychiatric issues made in counselling are clearly more difficult in some of these new modalities.

Changes have also taken place in non-statutory sectors. The pressure on voluntary sector organisations to follow the statutory sector in evaluation of outcomes, clinical governance and audit has both raised standards and also put considerable pressure on the staff and trustees of organisations who often have to develop these with no additional funding or resources. The growth of provision of counselling within the voluntary sector for those with particular medical conditions also has made medical support and liaison even more relevant. The independent sector has up to now been less subject to requirements in areas such as clinical governance but there are indications that this may change in the near future.

The Approach of this Book

There are many ways of covering the subject matter dealt with by this book and our particular approach is best outlined at the outset. One of the assumptions we have chosen to work within is the validity of psychiatry in the treatment of certain disorders which may come the counsellor's way. There are conditions which present mainly with psychological symptoms where counselling does not have a major contribution to make and, within this, a smaller group where it may be harmful. Clients may need medication and hospitalisation and in some cases, where the person's life or the life of others is at risk, these may need to be compulsory.

In relation to physical illness we accept that in most instances the causes are mainly physical or environmental and that the role of counselling is a peripheral one, both in prevention and treatment, except in relation to a limited number of conditions or for certain people. However, counselling can have an important role to play in a number of areas, such as assisting in helping a person to come to terms with what has happened to them and, in some cases, help in pain control. There can also be benefits in the reduction of stress, which can sometimes make relapse less likely and ongoing treatment more effective. The rationale for what follows is that the concerns of counselling and medicine, especially psychiatry, are closely related and that the counsellor needs to have a grounding of knowledge in these areas. This will not make the counsellor an expert, or equipped to make either diagnoses or recommendations about treatment. The intention is more to alert the counsellor to situations where advice or referral should be sought. It is important that we are all aware of our limits to competence, as required in most counsellors' codes of ethics and practice, and that we know what to do when we are faced with such situations.

Theoretical Perspective and Working Context

The counsellor's approach to any issue is very much influenced by the theoretical perspective within which she works. In the course of a short book it is not possible to deal with the issues from all the major theoretical perspectives, so a broad integrative approach is taken with some occasional reference to specific theories. This book may also reflect in parts a closer relationship between the activity of the counsellor and the client's GP than many counsellors practise. In the relationship between the client's counsellor and her GP our view is that contact and co-operation are at least desirable and often essential for the well-being of clients and we hope, without being over-prescriptive, to promote a re-think of ways of operating where this is appropriate.

Counsellors in primary care now also work alongside graduate workers in mental health. These are people who have completed a degree in psychology or other relevant discipline who have undergone a year-long training programme to equip them with the necessary skills to work with patients with brief cognitive-behaviourally informed techniques in such areas as guided self-help for depression and anxiety management. This book is primarily directed to those who operate within a clear counselling framework, but we hope that others, such as graduate workers, who use counselling as part of their work will also find it of value. However, it is important to recognise that particular problems attach to combining counselling with some other activities, such as advocacy, and it is beyond the scope of this book to explore these extensively. Some of the boundary issues that arise, however, form part of the discussion of ethics in Chapter 7. Much confusion surrounds the similarities and differences between counselling and psychotherapy. These terms are used synonymously by some and in a clearly different way by others, although with no consistency in the differences. One of the clearest differences between counselling and psychotherapy in our view is that counselling is a skills-orientated and problem-solving activity whereas psychotherapy is based more in theory and addresses issues wider than those that led to the referral, but practitioners from both fields encounter the kinds of issues raised in this book.

Summary

The next chapter looks at the basic common principles of care and of working with other professionals. We consider what is meant by mental illness, models of mental illness and the relationship between mental and physical health. Concepts of team-working in health care settings, the shortcomings of service delivery in the NHS and the problems that counsellors may face when working in medical settings are all introduced. Chapters 3 and 4 look at the way in which challenges to the counsellor's knowledge and skills may arise at various points in the counselling process and aim to help the counsellor think through situations and, where necessary, make decisions and take action. Chapter 3 examines both problems that arise at the point of referral and those that may happen during the process of assessment. It is important that the counsellor is able to have discussions with professional referrers (and with clients who self-refer) about the appropriateness of the referral that include taking account of relevant medical and psychiatric information. In assessment it is often important to be able to elicit and evaluate the client's past and present medical and psychiatric history before making any decision about ongoing counselling. Chapter 4 considers how to manage the situation where medical or psychiatric conditions emerge during the course of counselling, either because they occur part way through counselling, or because they have been hidden. There are also issues to address when illness or psychological disturbance occurs in the counsellor's own life.

Chapter 5 looks at medical conditions and their treatment in relation to counselling. Using the distinction between signs of illness that the counsellor can recognise, and the symptoms that clients may talk about, we then go on to discuss particular physical health problems which the counsellor can learn to recognise, and what sort of response to these the counsellor should make. Additionally, both the impact of medical conditions and treatments on counselling and the potential positive and negative effects of counselling are considered. Chapter 6 addresses psychiatric conditions and their treatment in relation to counselling. This is approached from the viewpoint of assessing the problems that the client presents, rather than from a starting point of diagnosis. Important aspects covered are helping the counsellor to recognise serious mental health problems and to understand the effects of drugs prescribed for psychiatric conditions.

The final substantive chapter deals with the ethical and legal issues that can arise around medical and psychiatric issues in the work of counsellors. An important part of this is trying to establish what the boundaries are to the counsellor's duty of care to clients in relation to their psychological and physical health. The ways in which this may vary according to the setting in which the client is seen are considered and relevant sections of the BACP Code of Ethics and Practice for Counsellors are identified and discussed. Ethical issues are becoming increasingly relevant as counselling seeks to further establish itself as a profession and clients become more aware of the standards they can expect from professionals and how to complain if they are not met.

Within the book is some duplication, overlap between chapters and direction to other chapters to facilitate its use as a reference book rather than just one that is read from cover to cover. For the same reason, we have also included in the glossary terms which are defined in the book, but not in every chapter where they are found. Whilst we have tried to give sound advice based on current understandings in the various disciplines that impinge on counselling in this context, we cannot be responsible for the way in which this information and guidance is used by practitioners. Throughout we stress the importance of counsellors having multiple sources of support and advice, particularly from medical and psychiatric sources, and especially in dealing with difficult situations.

2 Common Principles of Care and Working with Others

In this chapter we will explore the concepts that underpin clinical practice, and introduce certain ideas and themes to which we will return in later chapters.

What is Meant by 'Mental Illness'?

The differences between mental health and illness, and what is considered normal and abnormal in psychological terms, are perhaps not so easily determined in mental health care as in physical medicine. However, there are some principles that can be usefully applied. Generally, in medicine, the concept of a 'syndrome' is applied to a collection of symptoms that can be recognised as commonly occurring together in an identifiable pattern. When it is possible to further define an underlying biophysical process that can be demonstrated to cause this syndrome the term 'disease' is used. For most syndromes in physical medicine the term 'disease' can be applied. This is not so in psychiatry except in neuropsychiatric disorders, such as dementia, in which physical changes can clearly been seen in the structure of the brain. However, there is increasing evidence that biophysical processes in the brain play a part in the development of other disorders such as schizophrenia and severe depression.

So when does a psychiatrist use the term mental illness? This is generally when a clear syndrome can be identified and there has been a definite change from how the person used to be (which is important in differentiating illness from 'personality disorder' which is not viewed as 'illness') and there is a deterioration in the person's ability to function effectively. Dependence on alcohol or drugs is similarly not viewed as being mental illness. However, psychiatrists are often involved in treatment in these areas in order to attempt to relieve suffering either as experienced by the person themselves or those around them. We shall use the generic term 'serious mental health problems' to encompass serious mental illness, addictions and personality disorder. By serious mental illness we mean the presence of considerable loss of ability to function normally, or considerable suffering (often with the addition of delusions or hallucinations), or both. Personality disorder is a lifelong abnormality of relating to others, and psychiatrists have spent many years inventing categorical labels for abnormal personalities. However, people rarely fit one exactly and these labels should be used with some caution, as labels tend to be very sticky and the presence of a personality disorder does not preclude the additional development of mental illness. It is also important to note that most people, normal or abnormal, possess a number of different traits rather than neatly fitting into one category.

> Diane works in an agency which has a consultant psychiatrist attached to it. In the case of Fred, Diane referred the client to the psychiatrist for an assessment and report. The report on Fred was descriptive, simply saying that Fred is not mentally ill, and makes no treatment recommendations. Diane is convinced that Fred is quite disturbed but well motivated and Diane wants to help. In the case of this professional disagreement what can or should Diane do?
>
> A person can be significantly psychologically disturbed without having a formally diagnosable 'mental illness'. A common criticism of psychiatrists (frequently justified) is that they often limit their reports to an opinion about the presence or absence of 'mental illness' and then do not give any recommendations for what to do in the absence of this. The psychiatrist may consider that Fred has personality problems which may not be helped, or possibly exacerbated, by counselling if it is deeper than at a supportive level. In the first instance Diane should discuss the problem with the psychiatrist and ask for further clarification. If this is not forthcoming, the next step depends on the view of the organisation in which Diane works, as the matter should be raised with them. If this route is not satisfactory, Diane should encourage Fred to consult his GP and discuss the matter with a view to obtaining a second opinion.

This example also raises the issues of how psychiatrists perceive counsellors and how the counsellor should set about communicating with the GP or mental health professionals and we will return to these matters below.

A further complicating factor is that judgements about appropriateness of behaviour and beliefs are often made without due attention being paid to cultural context. Concern has been expressed about the tendency for more people from Afro-Caribbean culture to receive the diagnosis of schizophrenia in the UK when compared with people from other cultures. There is also evidence that people from Asian cultures tend to express depression more frequently in terms of physical symptoms than those from European cultures. These issues, however, remain controversial and are well explored from mainstream and more radical viewpoints in Rack (1982) and Fernando (2003), respectively.

This discussion may seem laboured, but the presence of defined mental illness has significance in law, both in considering an individual's responsibility for his or her actions and when compulsory detention or treatment is being considered under the Mental Health Act. The various 'sections' of the Act and their relevance are discussed in Chapter 6. Those interested in the concept of illness should consult Kendell (1975) and Clare (2001) for further discussion of this.

Models of Mental Illness

Psychiatry is a branch of medicine in which the 'symptoms' and 'signs' addressed relate to aspects of thought, perception, emotion, behaviour, intellect or personality rather than to bodily functions such as gastrointestinal functioning or respiratory functioning. As we shall see, the dividing line between psychiatric and physical disorders is not clear-cut, as the presenting symptoms of many physical disorders can be psychological and vice versa.

Various models of mental illness can be identified. In Table 2.1 we briefly discuss these models.

Table 2.1 Models of mental illness and mental health care

Model	Psychological			Social			
	Biological	Psychodynamic	Cognitive-behavioural	Stress models	Family models	Conspiratorial	Spiritual
Influences	Predominant basis of health professional training and the 'new genetics' Some support from carers	Remains a powerful model in lay terms though 'out of fashion' in health care provision	Powerful model in psychology and current mental health policy	Influential in thinking of social workers and in primary care	Influences social work, child and family work and primary care	Survivor groups, radical professionals and anti-psychiatrists	Religious belief
Causal models	Problems caused or mediated by physical changes in brain and/or neurochemical pathways	Understand behaviour in terms of early experiences	Inappropriate learning, poor coping skills	Social and cultural stress	Whole family is 'sick' person acts in response to family pressures	Myth of mental illness – result of way person is expected to behave by others	Variety of spiritual theories – depending on culture/religion
Treatment models	Drugs, ECT	Psychodynamic psychotherapy – one-to-one and group	CBT, BT, social skills training	Social change and interventions	Family therapy	None – empower and advocate for person who is labelled as mentally ill	Faith based therapies, retreat and meditation
Rights and duties of client/patient	Right to sick role but must co-operate	Responsible – but spared moral judgement	Responsible – contract to co-operate	Right to help but must co-operate	Whole family duty to participate	Right to privacy and same rights as others	Obligation depends on personal faith

Source: Adapted from Colombo et al. 2003

Each model has historically been supported by particular groups in the community (for example doctors or nurses) and can be linked to its own particular approach to causation, treatment methods and the subsequent roles and responsibilities of the client or patient (Colombo *et al.*, 2003). People often assume that psychiatrists only employ the biological model. This refers to a way of working that seeks physical causes in order to confirm the presence of 'disease'. It entails carrying out physical investigations, by methods such as using new developments in visualising the brain, for example by magnetic resonance imaging (MRI scanning) which have undoubtedly brought about a revolution in the understanding of how the brain functions. It also of course involves prescribing drugs and giving electro-convulsive therapy (ECT). The biological model is undoubtedly important, and this perspective is often that which a medically trained individual can exclusively provide. However, the psychological and social perspectives, which can be provided by a range of non-medically trained professionals, are seen as being of equal importance in terms of fully understanding the causes of a person's problems, what investigations to carry out and what treatment is required (for a fuller analysis see Anthony Clare's excellent book *Psychiatry in Dissent* [Clare, 2001]). Psychological approaches can be employed in conjunction with drug treatments and alongside practical social help, such as with housing problems. Counselling is never contraindicated in someone with serious mental illness; what must be considered is the appropriate level of work, which we will return to later.

In understanding an individual and his or her problems, no single model can provide all the answers. Experienced mental health workers of all professions learn the value of eclecticism and the importance of working as part of a team. This applies within both primary and specialist mental health care so that best use can be made of the knowledge and skills each member has to offer.

Mental and Physical Health

The French Philosopher René Descartes was the first to clearly identify the mind with consciousness and self-awareness and to distinguish this from the brain, which was seen as the seat of intelligence. Hence, he was the originator of the 'Cartesian' mind/body split in the form in which it still exists today. Although this concept has been very influential in the development of modern scientific thinking, it is actually rather unhelpful when attempting to understand how people present with emotional problems in everyday primary care. The mind and body are intimately connected, and lay models of health care in almost all cultures do not distinguish mind from body. Thus it is understandable to most people that a person with an emotional problem might experience physical symptoms. The concept of 'stress' resulting in physical symptoms as well as emotional ones is widely appreciated. The problem, however, arises when the person consults their doctor because of worries that there may be a physical cause (which indeed there might also be) and the doctor only considers the potential organic diagnosis without also looking at the emotional factors that might be playing a part. The ways in which physical and emotional health problems may be intertwined are considered in Table 2.2.

Table 2.2 Relationships between mental and physical illness

Relationship	Examples
Mental disorder may provoke physical illness	Depression most likely to do this Stressful life event→depression→physical illness Anxiety may also, e.g. anxiety provoking episode of asthma, migraine
Psychiatric symptoms may be presenting symptoms of a physical illness	Thyrotoxicosis (over-active thyroid) may present with anxiety. An under-active thyroid may present as depression
Mental illness may be the direct consequence of physical illness	Anxiety or depression as a result of development of an illness Depression is very common in the presence of chronic illness such as diabetes and arthritis, but can also occur as a result of cancer
Mental illness may exacerbate the pain of a physical illness	People who are depressed experience pain as more severe than when they are well. This holds for any chronic pain, for example back pain
Mental illness may present as physical illness	Such symptoms may be the common physical symptoms of emotional distress, e.g. physical symptoms of anxiety such as palpitations, or weight loss associated with depression – or they may be otherwise 'medically unexplained' – a phenomenon known as 'somatisation'

How Common is Mental Illness in the Community?

Depending on which sets of criteria are used in research, around 4–13% of the population have mental illness at any one time (Bird/Mental Health Foundation, 1999). However, there is now more or less international agreement on, for example, what constitutes depression or schizophrenia. In the course of a year, 12 million adults attending GP surgeries in the UK have psychiatric symptoms (mostly of anxiety and/or of depression). Only 1 in 10 of those so recognised by the GP is referred to a psychiatrist and only 1 in 100 is severely enough depressed to require admission to hospital. About 40% of those with depression are not recognised by the GP as being depressed, largely because they also have physical illness which the doctor focuses on exclusively, or because they present with somatic symptoms of emotional distress.

For reasons that are still not entirely clear, more women than men receive a diagnosis of mental illness, although men are selectively more likely to be referred to secondary care services. Women are more likely to consult the doctor for all symptoms not just emotional ones, and men are much less likely do so, certainly between the ages of 20 and 40. When they do consult, GPs seem to have a higher threshold for diagnosing that a man has a mental health problem and as a result problems have often become more severe by the time that they are recognised. Men who are depressed may more likely turn to alcohol and other drugs to self-medicate than seek help and may present with addictions and behavioural disturbances such as 'uncontrollable anger' rather than depression and anxiety.

Measuring the Severity of Emotional Distress

A number of different tools or rating scales have been used in both research and everyday practice to measure the severity of emotional distress. Some of these can also be used to 'screen' for the presence of emotional problems and some can be used at intervals to assess progress over time and to provide an objective measure of outcome. They are increasingly used in NHS practice in the UK in order to provide evidence of the effectiveness of therapies, including counselling, and some rating scales are now being used by GPs to assess the severity of depression in people with newly presenting symptoms, in return for payment under the new GP contract (see below).

Measures in common use are summarised in Table 2.3.

Table 2.3   Measurement tools

Measurement tool	Use	Find at:
CORE (Clinical Outcomes in Routine Evaluation)	Now commonly used in counselling and psychotherapy services	www.coreims.co.uk Free to download scales, but other services for subscribers
PHQ-9 (Personal Health Questionnaire-only depression) GAD-7 (new for anxiety)	Increasingly used in primary care services. Recommended for use by GPs for assessment of depression	www.depression-primarycare.org/clinicians/ toolkits/materials/forms/phq9/ questionnaire/ Free to download
BDI (Beck Depression Inventory)	Used now more in research, but also recommended for GPs	Costs for use www.nfer-nelson.co.uk/education/resources/ cat3/cat3.asp
HADS (Hospital Anxiety and Depression Scale) Measures anxiety and depression	Designed to use in presence of physical illness, which might confound measurement. Also recommended for GPs	
GHQ (General Health Questionnaire) Not specific for anxiety or depression – general measure of distress	Primarily used in research. Widely translated. 12, 28, 30 and 60 item versions	

Professionals Involved in Assessing and Treating Mental Health Problems

Psychiatrists are medically qualified and undergo a further minimum of six years' postgraduate training prior to appointment as a consultant in the NHS. Some psychiatrists work in association with Community Mental Health Teams (CMHTs) and a minority also work in close liaison with GPs in primary care settings. Although all members of the Royal College of Psychiatrists (essential for consultant status) are expected to have received some training and supervision in psychotherapy, few have achieved a high level of expertise either in psychodynamic or behavioural therapies and this tends to be the case only for those who are appointed as Consultant Psychotherapists. Referral is generally only possible via the person's GP or another doctor. Many NHS consultants also have sessions as part of a private practice.

Psychotherapists come from a range of backgrounds. Those employed within the health service can be psychiatrists who have undergone further training in psychotherapy or they may come from one of the other professions allied to medicine. Many psychotherapists also work in private practice and for non-statutory organisations concerned with the care of people with mental health problems (e.g. Philadelphia Association, Arbours Association). All psychotherapists working within both the public and private sectors can now apply for UKCP recognition which guarantees that they have achieved a degree of training approved by the UK Council for Psychotherapy (www.psychotherapy.org.uk). The British Confederation of Psychotherapists is a separate organisation consisting solely of psychoanalysts and psychoanalytic psychotherapists.

Community Mental Health Nurses (also known as Community Psychiatric Nurses (CPNs) are qualified Registered Mental Nurses who work outside the hospital setting, often as members of a Community Mental Health Team. Some also have close liaison with primary care. Although specific training for work in community settings does exist in the form of diploma courses, not all CPNs have undergone such training. CPNs have not usually received any training in counselling or psychotherapy before qualification, although GPs often assume they are qualified to 'counsel'. Direct referral to CPNs from primary care or other agencies is often (but not always) possible. Behavioural nurse specialists are psychiatric nurses who have completed specialised training in behavioural therapy. Sometimes they work alongside clinical psychologists or independently take referrals directly from GPs. They do not necessarily have experience of community psychiatric nursing.

Social Workers (SWs): The majority of social workers in the mental health field have the CQSW (Certificate of Qualification in Social Work) and work as part of a CMHT, a Local Authority Area Social Services Team or in other specialist areas such as Child Guidance Clinics or Community Alcohol Teams. Social Workers with specific training and experience in mental health problems who have special powers under the Mental Health Act (see Chapter 6) are known as Approved Social Workers (ASWs). Most social workers have training in basic counselling skills and a minority have specific psychotherapy training, often in fields such as family or couple relationship therapy. A small number of SWs (fewer than in the past) have close links with GPs. Social workers can take referrals from a range of agencies and individuals.

Clinical Psychologists have a degree in psychology and a postgraduate qualification (usually a doctorate) in psychology. As part of their course all will have learned about all aspects of psychological assessment and treatment, but their specific expertise will depend on their experience and therapeutic orientation, e.g. behavioural, cognitive, neuropsychological, psychodynamic. Some are members of CMHTs and some liaise closely with GPs. Direct referral is generally possible without first referring to the psychiatric service.

Occupational Therapists work throughout the health service in a range of settings. Those who work in mental health are based in hospitals or in the community, often in a CMHT and have training and experience in group skills and usually also in counselling skills. Referral is via the psychiatric service.

Community Mental Health Teams (CMHTs): In many areas, mental health professionals in the community work as a team and all referrals in that area are preferably made not to individual professions, but to the 'team' who then decide on who has the most appropriate skills to take the assessment forward. The majority of teams have a psychiatrist as a member, but the input of clinical psychologists is variable and the reorganisation of community care has tended to threaten the provision of social workers in such teams. They may vary from taking referrals only from GPs to a broader range of referrals from agencies in the community and self-referrals.

General Practitioners: In order to be a principal in general practice it is necessary to have undergone Vocational Training which involves three years' training following medical registration, one of which is as a trainee in a general practice. Experienced older GPs often have not undergone this training and of those who are vocationally trained only 40% have any specific experience in psychiatry beyond what they learned at medical school. GPs have a variable knowledge of counselling, although younger doctors will have received communication skills training at medical school and as a trainee, often employing the use of video, role-play or actors. It has been demonstrated that although there has been a growth in the number of people employed as counsellors within general practice, a significant minority of GPs do not sufficiently understand what they do, those for whom counselling would be appropriate, or what are the qualifications of counsellors (Sibbald *et al.*, 1993).

Practice nurses are Registered General Nurses who are employed directly by GP practices and will have had a diversity of experience. Although some are expected to provide 'anxiety management' or 'counselling', few have adequate training or supervision, although most do see people with mental health problems in their everyday work. Practice nurses conduct most of the reviews of people with chronic illness, particularly diabetes, and thus may actually see many people with anxiety and/or depression associated with chronic illness without having the skills to detect or treat these problems. However, this may change in the new GP performance related payment system in the UK (the Quality and Outcomes Framework; QOF) where GPs are getting payment specifically for the detection of depression in people with diabetes and cardiovascular disease in clinics usually run by the nurse.

Health Visitors are Registered General Nurses with a further qualification in health visiting. They play a key role in the recognition of post-natal depression and some have received specific training in counselling to help them in managing this particularly common form of depression.

Graduate Mental Health Workers (or Primary Care Mental Health Workers) were introduced in the UK to improve access to psychological therapies in the primary care setting. They usually have a degree in psychology or other social science and have completed a one-year diploma course in primary care mental health. The content of these courses varies around the UK. Their work incorporates direct contact with clients offering brief psychological interventions, such as guided self-help and signposting clients to appropriate community agencies, in addition to audit and development work in primary care (Bower, 2002). So far the degree to which integration with primary care has been achieved has been very variable.

Communicating with Other Professionals – and the Client

Good communication is crucial to the provision of quality mental health care. However, in practice all the professionals involved may treat each other with some suspicion and view counsellors as impinging on their territory. It will be easier for the counsellor to relate to the primary care team if he or she works in such a setting, but this may be more difficult if they work elsewhere. Whether or not such communication actually takes place will depend on the nature of the therapeutic contract with the client and the setting and nature of the problem posed by the client's mental state. The ethical implications around communicating with other professionals are discussed in Chapter 7. Where the client works outside the primary care setting he or she may in most cases simply advise the client to seek further help from the GP, but a short communication to acknowledge why this has been advised can be very helpful.

In any communication with another professional it is important for the counsellor to describe succinctly the problem they are concerned about, how the client came into their care, the terms of their therapeutic contract, including aims and goals and what they would like the GP or psychiatrist to address. It is also crucially important to say exactly what they have said to the client. This can open up channels of communication between professionals and between professionals and the client.

Working as a Team

It is common for staff from different professional backgrounds to have strong views about the value of their own and of others' work. Mental health workers and primary care staff vary in their attitudes towards counselling depending on their own training and orientation to biological or more holistic perspectives. Some feel that counsellors may miss physical disorders in clients who present to them, whilst others recognise that there is no rational need for competition given the level of need for skilled psychological help in the community. There is, however, a realistic concern that all counsellors should be able to recognise when they have reached the limits of their training and expertise in helping someone with more complex problems.

Some Important Principles of Teamwork

It is easy when a client moves across the interface from one service to another for some 'splitting' to occur whereby communication does not occur or professionals come to see each other as rivals, incompetent, or not behaving professionally.

Effective communication, respect for the expertise of others and an emphasis on the shared goal of client care can facilitate effective referral, as can a positive pre-existing relationship. Often the client can take responsibility for both the choice of referral and for explaining why they felt this was needed, and this should ameliorate any inter-professional difficulties. Emphasis on the therapeutic contract and areas which will continue to be held confidential may help reassure clients, and set clear boundaries for the details given in referral. Staff may find it useful to copy the client into letters so that there is no mystery or confusion about what has been written to whom. It is now the policy in the NHS for patients and clients to be offered the option of receiving copies of correspondence about their healthcare.

The Changing Care Pathway

A number of new roles have been developed in recent years in mental health services and primary care teams are also altering their skill mix. This can be confusing for counsellors and their clients who are not updated on changes to service configurations. Counsellors can improve their service knowledge by the use of NHS websites and the information provided for patients by local services. Primary care teams now have websites and an e-mail address whereby simple queries can be put directly to GPs or nurse practitioners. Counsellors might think about using these for queries about whether and how to refer, or perhaps to agree a time when a telephone discussion could occur. Mental health services usually have a standard referral form which will specify where the form should be sent and often also the range of possible assessments that will follow. Graduate health workers are usually skilled in offering advice on local self-help services and self-help strategies, although counselling clients will probably be beyond this level in terms of need. There are now, in most localities, crisis teams who can act quickly when clients with more severe mental illnesses become highly symptomatic, and there is usually group therapy available which could be useful to complement counselling if, for example, symptomatic anxiety or compulsive behaviours are a recurrent barrier to improving social integration. There are always risks to referral while a client is engaged in therapeutic work, but the reasons for referral can be to complement treatment as well as to assess physical or psychiatric problems.

Deficiencies and Limitations in Mental Health Services

A major problem is the emerging lack of services serving the gap between primary care, led by the GP team, who are able to manage fairly uncomplicated problems of anxiety and depression, and the community mental health services (focused on the CMHT) which are increasingly focused on people with psychotic disorders. This means that people with more complex but non-psychotic problems, such as severe depression, personality difficulties, and people with generally messy lives and often poor coping styles are not well served by specialist care, even though they may pose a degree of risk to themselves or others because of their distress. Mental health services are often reluctant to take on these clients, perceiving them as not having 'severe and enduring mental illness'. As a consequence, mental health workers in other settings, particularly primary care, may feel 'dumped on' and asked to manage people who really need more resources, or a different form of help than they can offer within a counselling relationship. It is extremely important, and indeed one of the major principles of this book, that counsellors should not feel that they cannot challenge assessments made by other mental health workers that have been more influenced by resources rather than risk. It is important to recognise that there are limits to what can be safely and properly contained within a counselling relationship or contract.

Summary

Good practice in working with others for the benefits of clients requires some knowledge of their role, respect in principle for the expertise which they can offer, and effective communication in a suitable format which is agreed with the client which leads to the hoped for response rather than confusion. The active agreement of the client is crucial, as they can then lead the referral rather than being passive while professionals agree (or disagree) over their heads. The fears of clients that counsellors are rejecting them when referrals are made should be a focus of therapeutic discussion and counsellors should endeavour to keep the existing therapeutic contact with the client while they are seeking other help elsewhere. All the normal rules of confidentiality should apply to referrals just as they would for a client and their social networks. Later chapters will consider other challenges to the effective use of clinical services.

3 Issues at the Beginning of Counselling

Introduction

The processes surrounding the referral and assessment of clients for counselling are complex and the difficulties increase considerably where medical and psychiatric conditions are part of the client's situation. The basic decision that has to be made by the end of the assessment process is whether counselling is appropriate to the person's circumstances and needs and can be offered safely and competently by the counsellor. Sometimes there is pressure to make an immediate positive response, such as when a GP who wants to make a referral asks for advice or a decision over the telephone, or in passing in the corridor. It is important to resist this as the decision about whether counselling will be offered can only be the outcome of a thorough assessment. However, it is important to bear in mind that it can be very disappointing for clients to be referred and assessed and then turned down as unsuitable for further sessions. Because of this it is good practice to try to ensure that referrers do not create unrealistic expectations in their patients and that people seen for initial appointments will benefit, either from a one-off session or from regular counselling.

Managing Referrals

It is not uncommon to receive a referral letter which has very sketchy details about the potential client, but with enough information to raise the counsellor's concerns about possible psychiatric or medical complexities and to create doubts about whether the person will prove suitable for counselling. In certain situations, such as where the counsellor and referrer work together on an ongoing basis, or in the independent and voluntary sector, the use of a standard referral form can be helpful. This should provide basic information about the person, the reasons for the referral, why the referrer thinks counselling would be of benefit, and any current medical or psychiatric conditions and medication.

Where such a system does not operate we will sometimes need to contact the referrer for more information before arranging to see the client. Generally an explanation of why the referral has been made and how the referrer believes the person will benefit from counselling will be more useful than further details about the person's problems or history. The counsellor may also usefully pick up in such a discussion with the referrer what the client has been told to expect and the extent to which this is likely to be a help or a hindrance in facilitating a positive attitude to counselling. One of the risks of going down this path of gaining more information about the referred person is that the issues become less clear or more complex. There is also a danger that, however much we try to resist it, we take on board something of other people's opinions and judgements in a way that clouds the assessment of the client when this eventually takes place. An additional hazard is that referrers are often in busy jobs and much time and energy may be consumed in trying to telephone them and unhelpful delays may ensue if the matter is conducted by e-mail or post. Despite any difficulties, establishing good channels of communication with any other professionals who may be involved with the person is important.

> Judith was referred by her GP for help with her current difficulties. The letter also mentioned that she suffered from a long-standing manic-depressive condition. Alan was uncertain whether this was an appropriate referral and did not want to raise the client's hopes of obtaining help if these were to be dashed. Contact with the GP established that her psychiatric condition was well-controlled and that she was looking for some help to work through some current issues at work and to consider a career change. On the basis of this an assessment session was arranged and ten sessions agreed to focus on these areas.

Referrers' Agendas

One of the situations the counsellor needs to safeguard against is where clients are referred because the person at present helping them has not thought out clearly the reason for the referral, just does not know what to do with the person or, worse, thinks it is someone else's turn to put up with them for a bit! Some may be tempted to think that if the request is coming from a medical source (or any another equally respected profession) then it must be a good idea. However, referrals from a medical source may be no more informed than those from other sources, and sometimes less so. For example, some GPs have unrealistic ideas of the timescale that would be involved in resolving long-standing and intractable problems through counselling and may expect such issues to be resolved in six or ten sessions. It is important for us to fully recognise the limits to our competence and not to allow professional judgement to be distorted by pressure or flattery. Rather we need to recognise that we have a part to play in educating other professionals about the value and limitations of counselling, which is still needed despite the widespread provision of counselling. Sometimes the outcome of the discussion with referrers will be to encourage them to consider alternative routes of referral, such as to psychiatrists, community psychiatric nurses, or social workers.

An important aspect in considering the referral may be whether any current psychiatric or medical input will continue alongside the work of the counsellor. There are considerable benefits where the counsellor can proceed with the knowledge that others are taking responsibility for particular areas of the client's care. The potential disadvantage of this is that, without clear boundaries in place which are kept to by all involved, there may be unclear areas of responsibility and input leading to confusion, or the playing-off of one professional against the other by the client.

The following example illustrates how service pressures may lead to counsellors being asked to see patients without adequate medical cover.

> One of the GPs contacted Alan, the GP counsellor, asking him to see Ray, a man in his thirties who had multiple problems. He presented at surgery with suicidal intentions after his wife suddenly left him. He also had a history of alcohol and drug problems and had been unpredictably violent in the past, in one instance towards a health professional. The GP was having difficulty obtaining an urgent psychiatric assessment for him and asked the counsellor to see him to hold the situation until this could be arranged. Alan, who had just qualified and had little experience of such problems, felt overwhelmed but found it hard to refuse and said he would think about it and let the doctor know. Fortunately he had a supervision session the next day at which the issues were fully explored. It quickly became clear that this was not a suitable referral at Alan's stage of experience and perhaps not for anyone. The supervisor helped Alan to be able to go back to the doctor and give a clear explanation of why the referral was not appropriate.

Table 3.1   Sample information sheet for referrers

Valley Counselling Crookes Valley Grove Sheffield S10 4KI
0114-322-5091 (9 - 5 weekdays) e-mail: valleycounsel@psychprovider.com

The Valley Counselling Agency is a voluntary sector service for the community which has been established in Sheffield for nearly twenty years. We are widely used by the NHS, social services and other organisations and also accept self-referrals. We offer mainly short-term individual work using an integrated approach – generally ten weekly sessions. The service operates to high professional standards and all our counsellors have obtained, or are working towards, accreditation with the BACP.

We offer counselling for a wide variety of difficulties and can advise about the suitability of a possible referral if you would like to ring us. In practice we mainly see people experiencing difficulties with anxiety, depression or in their relationships, but we also commonly work with those experiencing eating disorders, the consequences of sexual abuse and other problems. The kind of counselling we offer looks at both people's present situation and their past history where this is relevant. We do not charge fees, but clients are invited to make a donation for each session.

Our aim is to offer an assessment appointment within ten working days and to offer regular appointments within two months of the assessment. Every effort is made to offer appointment times that are convenient, but waiting times may be longer if someone's availability is restricted. Where a formal referral is made, a short report is sent to the referrer following the assessment. It is also our policy, with clients' consent, to inform GPs when they begin and end their period of counselling with us.

The kind of counselling we offer usually requires that others are not involved in giving similar help. We do recognise, though, that there may be a need for complementary help, for example in the form of medication. Where other professionals are involved we, with clients' consent, liaise with them and try to foster a co-operative working relationship in the best interests of clients.

Before the assessment appointment clients are sent a pack of information about our agency, including clear directions about how to find us. At this first appointment the counsellor obtains as clear a picture as possible of the person's difficulties. Following this an explanation of any counselling that is proposed is given, including any risks or alternatives. Clients are encouraged and helped at this interview to set their own aims and to ask questions about the service and any help that is being offered or proposed.

Please feel free to contact us if you need to know more about our service or have any questions.

John Wilmott
Service Manager

Successful multi-professional involvement needs not only clear boundaries, but also good communication within a context of mutual trust between all involved. These dilemmas arise as much for those who work in medical settings as for those working in other sectors (Higgs and Dammers, 1992: 34). These issues were explored in Chapter 2.

The Influence of Setting

Alongside the nature of clients' problems and counsellor competence, the other major factor in making decisions at assessment is the particular setting in which the counsellor is working. Clients sometimes approach those working in the voluntary or independent sector because they wish to avoid involvement with the medical profession and assume that no liaison with their GP will be needed. Some have a fear or mistrust of doctors which may be leading them to neglect their physical or mental health. More commonly, people are anxious to avoid having issues relating to psychological health on their medical records because they rightly or wrongly anticipate that this will negatively affect their future career prospects. On the other hand, counsellors in primary care may particularly see those who tend to turn to their doctor for help as a first preference.

John came for an initial appointment after being persuaded by some friends to look for help. His main complaints were of social isolation and difficulties in making relationships, but in the course of the session he revealed that he believed that personal messages were being sent to him via his television. Anna also discovered that he was not registered with a GP and was not open to the idea of doing so or of having any contact with the medical profession in relation to his problems. Despite the potential pitfalls, Anna judged that John's interests were best served by offering him counselling. Important considerations in this were that at least he would have some form of therapeutic help and that it seemed unlikely that refusal would lead to him seeking more appropriate help. This counsellor felt able to take him on for counselling because she had access to medical advice and had previous experience in counselling clients with psychotic illness.

Some counsellors working in the independent or voluntary sectors may have chosen to work there in part because of their own negative views of the medical profession and of treating emotional and psychological problems in a medical context. Similarly some of those working within the NHS may have developed a very medicalised view of counselling. In dealing with clients it is important that we are aware both of our own personal values and prejudices, and of the pressures of the culture of the organisation within which we work and seek to deal with clients independently of these.

Medical Settings

There are a number of particular dilemmas that occur in medical settings. One of these is that people come for counselling because this is what a doctor says is needed rather than because they see the relevance for their particular problems. Many patients are very deferential to doctors even when they do not agree with what is being proposed. For example, some may go to see their GP for medication for depression or anxiety, but end up being referred to the practice counsellor instead. Because this is not what they want they may then try to enlist the support of the counsellor against the GP's assessment of what is appropriate. The counsellor may even find herself in a dilemma where she agrees with the GP's idea about what is appropriate, but recognises that no treatment is going to be effective without the co-operation of the client.

Tom was referred to Alan, a GP counsellor, for help with his depression. Exploration of the difficulty experienced by the counsellor in establishing a working relationship revealed that Tom had gone to his GP for anti-depressants. He did not want counselling, but in the face of the GP's decision had not seen any alternative to being compliant. Alan encouraged him to go back to the GP to discuss his treatment further. He also brought up at the next practice meeting the importance of referrals for counselling being made with patients' informed consent and understanding.

Another difficulty arises when we think that the patient's physical symptoms have not been fully explained or the patient feels they are not being taken seriously enough. Hopefully a situation will exist where such matters can be discussed constructively between the counsellor and the GP, but if this is seen as a challenge to the GP's judgement then difficulties in inter-professional relationships can ensue.

Tim went to see his GP convinced that his erectile problems had a medical cause and wanting Viagra. He was referred to John, the practice counsellor, as the GP thought there was nothing physically wrong and that the problem was caused by Tim's work stress. John found it very hard to engage Tim in counselling and it became clear that he was being compliant only to try to find a route back to medical treatment. It also became clear that Tim had a number of symptoms he was currently worried about and had been for various investigations in the past two years without physical causes being identified.

In response to this he had been trying a number of alternative therapies, some of them without checking whether the practitioner was appropriately trained and registered. In particular John was concerned about Tim's complaints that the chest pain that he had been experiencing over the last year had become worse and was 'different'. John discussed this with the GP who said: 'He's always complaining about his symptoms changing or getting worse and wanting new investigations. He needs to deal with the problems at work which he just will not face'. John was left uncertain about how to manage the situation.

Other Settings

Services which address the issue of psychological well-being in the workplace should normally provide a service of identifying patterns of referral of difficulties where the underlying dynamics are from the work setting. It is important in such cases that the clients referred are not individually pathologised through the applying of mental health labels or by issues being dealt with solely in counselling when they need to be addressed through other routes. Such routes may include occupational health, human resources departments, unions, professional bodies, legal advice and organisational feedback to the workplace. Similar issues can also arise in counselling for organisations offering employment assistance programmes and which either employ counsellors directly, or refer to counsellors in independent practice. Also, under such programmes, the maximum number of sessions provided for clients can be as little as six and this raises serious difficulties in addressing the needs of clients with serious and well-established mental health problems. It is also common practice for part of the agreement for those in independent practice to be that they cannot continue with clients needing long-term help even if clients themselves are willing to pay. This can create frustrations for both the counsellor and the client where a good working relationship had been established.

Independent practitioners also face the danger of isolation which can lead to a drift into bad habits and unsafe practices. Extra effort is often needed to ensure updating on professional and clinical matters and adequate channels for consultation and advice on medical and psychiatric issues. The latter is also important for voluntary sector and community organisations providing counselling. In addition, depending on the background and knowledge base of trustees, there may not be an appreciation of the clinical skills needed to effectively manage the service and not just as part of the clinical work with clients. There may also not be an understanding of the degree of professionalism needed to manage risk and provide a secure setting for vulnerable clients. Those who work with young people, for example in schools and colleges, need to be aware that particular legislation applies to those under 18 and those under 16 and this will be relevant to their management of medical and psychiatric dilemmas with these groups of clients.

Services Accepting Self-Referrals

Helpfully some clients who self-refer will have already discussed this course of action with their doctor and enlisted their support in going ahead with exploring how counselling may be of benefit. However, this is not generally the case with those who come to counsellors who accept self-referrals and who as a result are regularly faced with clients whose psychiatrists, GPs or others know nothing about their wish for counselling. Moreover, the attitude of these clinicians to counselling in general, and to the possibility of counselling for their patients in particular, is often not known to either the client or the counsellor. Where a person is receiving psychiatric treatment, or there is a clear link between a person's physical illness and their request for counselling, it is clearly desirable that any counselling is carried out with the support of practitioners already involved.

It is generally reasonable to at least respond to an enquiry about counselling by arranging an initial assessment appointment without consulting any professionals who are already involved. In any event, some counsellors work in settings where appointments are made for assessment without the opportunity for any discussion about the person's problems, or reason for seeking counselling. However, it is not in general acceptable for a counsellor to approach a self-referred client's doctor, either to gauge the appropriateness of counselling or the practitioner's attitude to it, without permission from the enquirer. Asking the client to inform their other carers can ensure that they retain control and gives the opportunity to explain the reasons for seeking counselling.

> Sue referred herself for counselling and attended for an assessment appointment during one of her periodic crises. During the course of this session it became clear that Jean had been under the care of psychiatrists in the past, and had probably been diagnosed as having a serious mental illness. This, together with other aspects of her problems that emerged during the session led Alisha, the counsellor, to be unsure about whether counselling would be an appropriate response. Alongside discussing the matter with his supervisor, the counsellor, with the client's permission, contacted her GP to discuss the appropriateness of counselling. As a result of this it came to light that Jean had recently been seen by a psychiatrist who had felt that counselling would be helpful. This was valuable to Alisha in coming to a decision to offer a series of appointments to her.

Table 3.2   Sample liaison letter to GP

Valley Counselling Crookes Valley Grove Sheffield S10 4KI
0114-322-5091 (9 - 5 weekdays) e-mail: valleycounsel@psychprovider.com

Dr. H.K. Francis,
120, Waters Street,
Sheffield
S3 4IG

Dear Dr. Francis,

Mr. P.D. Atkinson d.o.b. 21.05.71
35, Amberley Street,
Sheffield S14 2JI

This man came to see me recently for counselling because he was feeling depressed and isolated. I understand that he has not been to see you about these difficulties and so I asked him whether I could write to you and he agreed.

   We have identified some clear areas that he wishes to work on which are aimed at improving his mood and giving him more confidence to be in contact with others. We have agreed to meet initially for six sessions with the possibility of continuing for further sessions if counselling is proving to be helpful. I hope that this arrangement is satisfactory as far as you are concerned, and have also encouraged him to see you should this prove necessary. If there is anything I ought to know, and if you do envisage any difficulties in my seeing him for counselling, I would be grateful if you would contact me.

Yours sincerely,

Jane Williams
Senior Counsellor

   Where contact with a GP or other doctor is indicated and the client is resistant to this, great skill is needed in managing the situation. If frustration and defensiveness becomes established on both sides it is difficult to find a way forward. Sometimes a sensitive and understanding exploration of the client's concerns can

Table 3.3 Sample letter to client refusing counselling

Valley Counselling Crookes Valley Grove Sheffield S10 4JI
0114-322-5091 (9 - 5 weekdays) e-mail: valleycounsel@psychprovider.com

Ms. H. Thompson,
45, Howard Street,
Rotherham
S. Yorks
S65 4FI

Dear Ms. Thompson,

As promised I am writing to you following our session on Wednesday to let you know my thoughts about your request for counselling. Your position is a quite complicated one and, as I said then, I needed more time to think about your situation and to ask for advice from one of my colleagues. My main concern is that at the moment you do not have the general support in your life to deal with the kinds of things that counselling might bring up.

As you have just moved from London you have not had the chance to make many friends and have not yet made contact with a GP here. I think that it would not be very helpful for you to go back from sessions here to spend most of your week in a flat on your own. I do understand your wish to find something different from the psychiatric help you have been receiving over the last five years and do not want to close the door to your getting help from us. I suggest that you register with a GP and discuss your needs with him or her, and also give yourself time to become more established here. I would hope that this may resolve some of your difficulties, as it is always lonely starting off in a new place. However, if after you have become used to this area you feel our service could help please contact me again and we can review your request.

Yours sincerely,

John Wilmott
Senior Counsellor

---

open up the way for permission to be given. In the event of an impasse being reached it is important that the counsellor does not feel forced into offering help without adequate medical liaison or cover.

Care Plans

Where a person is already receiving help from the mental health services an important issue arises concerning the relationship of any counselling to the treatment which is already established. Ideally there should be in existence a care plan for the client and it needs to be clear how the proposed counselling fits into this as part of a coherent approach. Where the help a person is receiving does not appear to be well organised or have no clear rationale, then we may need to act as a catalyst in bringing about some process, such as a case conference, to ensure a coherent approach. Care needs to be taken in this not to take a critical or crusading stance, and not to jump to conclusions about lack of provision on the basis of too little, or inaccurate, information. Without a clear care plan the client may be subject to confusion and to contradictory ideas from different carers. Fragmentation and conflict in the overall care that a client receives will be particularly problematic where they mirror the client's internal state. In cases of physical illness it is also desirable that there should be a well-thought-out approach, particularly where there are strong psychosomatic elements to the client's illness.

> Simran referred herself for counselling for depression and in the course of the first session it emerged that she was currently receiving treatment from a psychiatrist. Alan, the counsellor, wrote to her psychiatrist with a copy letter to the GP. The letter outlined the problems which Simran was looking to address through counselling and the way that the counsellor planned to approach these, and asked whether this would fit in with her current care plan. The psychiatrist replied saying that she thought that counselling would be very helpful for Simran at this point.

Access to Services

The issue of access to services for those with disabilities is a complex one, whether this raises physical issues such as wheelchair access, or less publicised problems such as hearing difficulties and low vision. These particular difficulties can be at least partly addressed fairly easily by acquiring a portable induction loop and by producing information in large type format. There can also be access difficulties arising from problems that make it difficult for potential clients to leave their home, such as agoraphobia, ME and fatigue disorders and carer commitments, and services need to consider in some circumstances whether home visits are possible.

Some communication may need specialist skills of the counsellor, such as being able to do signing. Particular issues arise in providing counselling for people who need interpreters to access services. Realistically these are only currently available for those seen in the statutory sector, but even here there are problems of resourcing and availability which can make it difficult to reliably establish regular sessions. The introduction of a third person into the room can create difficulties in establishing the usual counselling processes, particularly for psychodynamic counselling where, for example, transference issues become very complex. There may be issues of confidentiality where the interpreter forms part of the client's community or concerns that the sense of what the counsellor is saying is communicated sufficiently by interpreters who do not have an understating of the counselling process.

Problems caused by strokes, brain haemorrhage and head injury require specialist knowledge of the effect of such trauma on communication. Shorter sessions may be necessary for those whose concentration span or stamina is limited, and flexibility about the arrangement and cancellation of appointments for those whose health means their ability to attend fluctuates. The counsellor may need to learn for each individual client the effective means of adapting the counselling to fit their communication difficulties.

Counselling in Difficult Environments

Sometimes the medical or psychiatric problems of clients mean that counselling can only take place in a situation that makes it difficult to maintain the usual boundaries around the work, typically either in the client's home or in hospital. Working in a client's home involves trying to ensure that there are as few interruptions as possible. Sources of possible interruption include the telephone, intrusions from others living in the home, visits from family or friends and expected and unexpected calls from trades people and others. Some of these may potentially compromise the confidentiality of the arrangement.

Where sessions are arranged in a medical setting that is not under the counsellor's control, ideally a room needs to be made available where meetings can take place. With such an arrangement the assumption must not be made that all staff understand to respect the boundaries involved and can be relied on not to interrupt sessions. There is generally an understanding that clinical sessions can be interrupted in certain circumstances, e.g. an urgent need for equipment or notes stored in the room. A change in such understandings may be agreed but resisted in practice because it is experienced as a challenge to the culture of the department. Seeing clients on the ward poses additional problems of managing interruptions and explaining the presence of the counsellor to visitors who may turn up unexpectedly without compromising confidentiality.

In considering counselling in home or medical settings it is important to weigh up the predicted benefits of counselling with the risks and disadvantages caused by the difficult setting. These need to be clearly discussed with the client. Arrangements for more viable alternatives need to be thoroughly explored before being rejected. An assessment should be made of the aspects of the boundaries around the counselling that can be controlled and those that cannot or may not be able to be sustained, in particular confidentiality. In this it is important not to be over-optimistic and have clear ways of managing the difficulties that may be encountered. These need to be discussed and agreed with the client.

> Carol was at a critical point in her counselling when she had a car accident that left her with injuries that would affect her mobility for at least three months. Amina explored various possibilities of trying to enable her to attend for sessions, but in the end a combination of access and transport issues made this impossible. The counsellor did not normally see people in their own homes, but in this case thought it was important to try to continue the sessions without a long gap, and so discussed it with her supervisor. The supervisor was supportive of the plans and helped Amina look at the issues involved in setting it up. This included a suitable room in which to conduct the sessions, choosing a time to meet when people were not likely to call and agreeing with the client not to answer the telephone during sessions.

Rejecting Referrals

In order to justify not accepting a referral a counsellor must be convinced that to see the person, even for assessment, would be totally inappropriate or too potentially harmful, either to the client or the counsellor. One situation where this might need to happen is where the enquirer makes it clear that his definition of confidentiality precludes any contact between the counsellor and those already involved in treating him.

Bill and Sue, a couple in their mid-twenties, came for help with difficulties in their relationship. In the course of assessment it became clear that a paediatrician was seeing
them with their daughter to deal with a problem of soiling. From Sue's description
of their last appointment Anna concluded that the doctor was beginning to suspect
that the daughter's problem was connected to their difficulties as a couple, and
was beginning to work with them on relationship issues. Anna said that some clear
boundaries would need to be set up between this treatment and any proposed more
intensive couple counselling and that this would involve the paediatrician knowing
about the latter. Even after explanations and explorations of their resistance to this
contact, the couple were unwilling that anyone should know about their coming to the
counsellor and therefore no further sessions were possible.

Table 3.4   Referral checklist, particularly for referrals from other professionals

1. Has the referrer a rationale for counselling for the client?
2. What has the client been told to expect from the counselling by the referrer?
3. Has the referrer a clear idea of what counselling may achieve?
4. Is the referral made on the basis that the goal of the counselling will be an improvement in a
   physical condition?
5. What has the client been told by the referrer about what to expect from counselling? Is what
   has been said likely to prove helpful or unhelpful?
6. Are any expectations of counselling unrealistic?
7. Are there other equally or more appropriate alternatives which the referrer might consider?
8. Are there any obvious indications against counselling?
9. Is further information needed before making a decision about moving on to a face-to-face
   assessment with the client?
10. Are other professionals already involved and, if so, is the referral part of a thought-out care plan?

Table 3.5   Referral checklist, particularly for self-referrals

1. Do those who may be involved in the person's treatment already know about/support the possibility of counselling?
2. What reasons has the person for thinking counselling may help?
3. Is the goal of the counselling to be an improvement in a physical condition?
4. Is the person expecting counselling to cure an underlying psychiatric condition?
5. Do you observe or sense signs of underlying or hidden problems of a medical or psychiatric nature?
6. Are there physical or psychiatric conditions that may be precipitated by counselling? If so,
   is sufficient support available to deal with what might happen?
7. Have you access to the medical and psychiatric back-up needed to take this referral?
8. If help from others is already being offered, does counselling make sense as part of an overall
   care plan?

Another possibility for refusing a referral will be if we feel too much at risk, as
when someone has a history of violence towards health professionals. In some
instances the work setting of the counsellor may be the key factor in deciding
whether the person can be seen. Those working with comprehensive and accessible
medical back-up, or who can call on immediate help if personal safety is threatened,
may be in a position to consider referrals that those working in a more isolated or
less well-staffed setting may not.

Carrying Out the Assessment

Some counsellors prefer to work with clients in a way that allows issues to emerge over a period of time from the material that clients choose to disclose rather than asking questions or undertaking a formal process of assessment. Some may see this way of working in early sessions as integral to the theoretical basis for their work, for example from a client-centred or psychodynamic perspective. This way of working is unwise and carries unacceptable ethical risks (see Chapter 7) and is also increasingly at odds with generally accepted practice. At the other end of the spectrum there is a danger that we can expect too much precision from assessment processes and place too much reliability on results from questionnaires and assessment schedules. Counsellors have to accept that, even with the best assess-ment, situations may remain unclear, and as a result uncertainties about what to do have to be tolerated and monitored as the counselling proceeds.

In assessing a client for counselling it is most important to elicit any relevant information about current psychiatric and medical conditions and any medication that the client is taking. It is also valuable as part of general history taking to enquire about any past psychiatric episodes and any periods of depression or anx-iety that were dealt with by the GP or have gone untreated, along with past major or chronic physical illnesses. Some of this will form part of a good referral letter and clients will often reveal much of the relevant material without prompting. We need, though, to be able to lead the client into discussing these areas without on the one hand being too intrusive and adopting an interrogatory style, or on the other being too easily put off by bland or non-committal answers. In this, having an idea of the kinds of questions and comments that might facilitate the process is helpful.

Table 3.6 Possible assessment questions, existing recognised conditions

1. Have you ever discussed this with your doctor?
2. Have you had help with this in the past?
3. Are there any other people helping you at present?
4. Are you taking any tablets at the moment?
5. Do you have any problems with your health?
6. Have you ever had any serious illnesses or accidents?
7. Has your doctor ever suggested that you see someone else about this?

Undiagnosed Conditions

An area which is likely to raise particular concern is dealing with the possibility of conditions that exist but may as yet be undiagnosed. The counsellor cannot operate with the knowledge base and expertise of a psychiatrist or GP, but needs to be able to form a credible judgement about whether a recommendation or referral to see a medical practitioner is needed. Chapters 5 and 6 aim to give the knowledge needed to do this. Ultimately the guideline must be that, if the counsellor is in doubt, she should seek advice or recommend that the client consults her GP. There is a need for enough expertise to be proactive in identifying possible psychiatric features and to be able to give some consideration to physical symptoms. By this we mean that part of a counselling assessment is to identify the degree to which someone has depression, anxiety and panic states, obsessive and compulsive disorders and so on; and to discover any signs of major mental illness such as delusions. Although the counsellor usually cannot bring the necessary technical expertise to these areas, by gaining experience in knowing what is within his or her competence, the counsellor comes to recognise those areas that fall outside of it.

Having identified a particular problem, such as a moderate level of depression, it can then be difficult to know what to do about it. At what point does depression cease to be something that can and should be contained within counselling? How much should the counsellor be influenced by the client's wishes and by the kind of approach the counsellor thinks will be used by the person's GP or local psychiatric services? There are no definitive answers to such questions and in each individual case a decision often only emerges out of a careful consideration and balancing of interests and possible future scenarios. It is important to remember that assessment is not just something that takes place at the point of referral, but that counsellors need to be involved in an ongoing process of monitoring and assessment. This means that in some instances it is valuable and appropriate to wait and see what emerges once the counselling is under way. We also need to be aware that we might learn incidentally about worrying physical symptoms in clients that are completely unrelated to their presenting problems and for which a recommendation to seek a medical opinion might be needed.

Linda, a woman of twenty, was referred for counselling by her GP as a result of fights that were developing between her and her boyfriend. Whilst there were various reasons for tensions in the relationship, she described a preoccupation with violent fantasies and disturbing dreams in which violence and blood were predominant themes and she was the perpetrator. Careful questioning revealed these to be unusual, but with no indication that they were part of a psychotic illness. This also seemed to be the conclusion of the GP. A course of counselling was offered and she was put on the waiting list although some ambivalence was expressed and some interest in obtaining a second opinion from a psychiatrist. By the time she reached the top of the waiting list Linda was in the care of a psychiatrist, her fantasies having become more clearly delusional in the meantime, and counselling did not proceed.

Turning to the area of physical illness, as we have noted the counsellor probably has no particular expertise, but with some knowledge and experience can begin to recognise the kinds of ways in which psychological problems manifest themselves and, by recognising those that cannot easily be accounted for within a psychological framework, comes to recognise symptoms that may need investigation. This applies, for example, to some neurological conditions where the loss of concentration and memory is qualitatively different from that associated with, say, stress or depression. Striano (1988) discusses physical conditions which may present as psychological problems, and Cooper (1973) gives two case histories providing salutary lessons where physical illness was wrongly diagnosed as psychological disorder.

> Mary, a retired solicitor in her early sixties, was recommended to see a particular counsellor by a friend who had been helped by him. She complained of difficulties with her memory which, to the counsellor, did not seem to be the kind normally produced by anxiety, stress or depression. In addition Mary did not seem to have any of these problems and he suggested that she consult her GP about a neurological referral. This led to a diagnosis of pre-senile dementia in its early stages.

At the point of assessment, it is important to try to negotiate with the client an area of common understanding of what counselling might be able to offer in relation to a physical illness. In particular there is a need to avoid the situation where a client embarks on counselling with a totally unrealistic idea of its physically curative possibilities. This for some may be part of a denial of the physicality of the illness and its consequences, and we would be wise to try to avoid collusion with this kind of denial. On the other hand, such tendencies are there to a minor degree in most clients and may form part of what is worked with in the counselling, but without an unhelpfully gross idealisation of the counselling process. It has also to be acknowledged that, in many areas of physical illness, the value or otherwise of counselling is unclear. Therefore, in taking up a particular position in this area, we must be careful to recognise and give due weight to the situation where a client takes a different view from us. This is particularly so when the client's view would also be taken by some of our reputable colleagues.

The counsellor needs to keep up with current developments in the possible benefits of counselling to those with chronic illnesses. There is not space here to adequately review the literature but only to give a few examples. Interventions such as crisis counselling and work with families and in groups have been shown to reduce emotional distress in those suffering from chronic illness (Altschuler, 1997; Taylor and Aspinwall, 1990: 29). Counsellors using a behavioural approach need to be acquainted with the techniques which have been developed to help people with a wide range of conditions (Dryden and Neenham, 2004). For example, Pearce and Wardle's book (1989) includes contributions, amongst others, on hypertension, cardiac rehabilitation, head injury, chronic pain, diabetes and respiratory disease. Broome (1989) draws together contributions relating to the psychological understanding of a large number of illnesses and a wide range of possible psychological approaches are covered in the discussion of the psychological treatment of these. There has been a growth in the literature on counselling those with cancer and in conjunction with palliative care (e.g. Bayliss, 2004; Burton and Watson, 1988; Davy and Ellis, 2000; Thompson et al., 2001). Palmer and Dryden (1995) in their book on stress counselling discuss health and lifestyle interventions in relation to alcohol intake, blood pressure, caffeine intake, smoking and weight control. Pollin (1995) addresses the issues involved in working short-term with those having chronic illnesses. The place of hypnosis in the counselling of those with chronic illness is covered by Frank and Mooney (2002). There are also many publications available that can be recommended to clients (e.g. Johnson and Webster, 2002).

Conflicts of View

This brings us to the difficult problem of differences in opinion within and between professions. This was touched on above when we suggested that the particular kind of treatment for depression that a client might be offered by his GP or local mental health services might influence the outcome of the counsellor's assessment of a depressed client. Whilst the general direction has been towards increased respect between professions and viewpoints, we do need to recognise both that a proportion of medical practitioners have a negative view of counselling and that some counsellors have serious doubts about many standard ways of dealing with psychiatric disorders. In addition counsellors may be aware that, whilst some of their clients may need medication or sanctuary, the setting in which these might be offered could preclude them obtaining the counselling that they need alongside this.

If the client is going to need psychiatric input as well as counselling, then obviously it is in the client's interests to try to set up some forms of help that complement each other, and to avoid opposition and exclusive choice between the possibilities. In this it is helpful if the counsellor can try to develop good links and

---

Table 3.7 Sample letter to GP

Valley Counselling Crookes Valley Grove Sheffield S10 4JI
0114-322-5091 (9 - 5 weekdays) e-mail: valleycounsel@psychprovider.com

---

Dr. F. D. Mason,
The Vale Medical Centre,
Spring Vale Walk,
Sheffield
S6 4IR

Dear Dr. Mason,

Mr. M.J. Fitzpatrick d.o.b. 03/06/70
24, Rowbuck Avenue
Sheffield S6 4EI

I am writing to you about this man whom I believe is one of your patients. He came to me recently asking for counselling help with his anxiety, for which he says he has received medication from you a few months ago. With his permission I am contacting you on two counts; firstly to check out that you have no objections to my seeing him for ten weekly sessions of counselling and secondly, with his permission, to share my concerns about some physical symptoms which he described to me.

He reports that for the last two weeks he has been suffering from headaches and dizzy spells. I realise that these may be related to the stress he is undergoing at work which is leading him to experience high levels of anxiety. However, I have suggested that he comes to see you about these new symptoms and also wanted to let you know directly about my concerns.

Yours sincerely,

Jo Smith
Counsellor

relationships with the relevant professionals in the community. It is important to recognise that the level of expertise and range of treatment options available from mental health services can vary greatly on a geographical basis, even within a city. Most practitioners will respond well to an approach from a counsellor who deals with matters in a professional manner and seeks to foster a co-operative working environment. They do not respond well to counsellors who try to tell them what to do or who reveal a hostile attitude to the ways in which they work with their patients or subject them to 'labelling'!

In making a referral or liaising with other professionals it is important to obtain the client's consent and not to behave in ways that are going to undermine their trust. Part of that is to keep them informed of the steps that you have taken and to discuss with them at each stage the reasons for your actions and the possible outcomes. Some counsellors consider it good practice to show their clients what they have written about them as part of referral or liaison, or to provide them with copies of the letters sent in settings where this is not normal practice. For the counsellor working within primary care, hospital or psychiatric settings, these concerns are often more easily dealt with as the understanding is likely to be that there is contact and liaison between various members of the team. There may be a different problem, however, of the counsellor not being able to establish a strong enough boundary around the counselling if other team members feel entitled to know what is going on in the counselling and to act upon such information as they see fit.

We also need to be aware that some other professionals have serious doubts about the effectiveness of counselling, or of a particular form of counselling, and may have concerns that it could actually do harm (Eysenck, 1992). These concerns may apply to either physical or psychological states and can in certain instances be well-founded. Particularly with psychotic states and serious physical illness there may not be benefits to be gained from working in a way that undermines psychological defences and increases a person's awareness of the underlying psychological state (see also Chapter 6). Such clients may benefit more from kinds of help that focus their minds on the external world rather than on internal states.

Alejandro came for an assessment appointment asking for help with fears about losing control of himself which seemed to the counsellor to be delusional. Taking a history from him revealed that he had been under the psychiatric services for many years, was on medication and was still seeing a psychiatrist for occasional appointments. A picture also emerged of someone socially isolated and finding it hard to cope with relationships. The counsellor felt that it was necessary to discuss the situation with his GP and obtained Alejandro's permission to do this. The GP advised against an approach that would explore and concentrate his attention on the delusional ideas, but was supportive of a short period of counselling focused on his social difficulties. The counsellor decided to accept this advice and offered Craig six sessions to work on this area, which he accepted and from which he benefited.

Referring On

One outcome of the assessment session may be that the client needs to be referred on and it is important to try to achieve this without the client feeling rejected or demoralised. People understandably tire of having to repeat their story to a number of professionals before they are able to find the right place to obtain help. If the session has gone well there is likely to be disappointment at not being able to see the counsellor again. This may be offset by the counsellor helping the client to recognise what has been achieved in the one session. It is also important for the counsellor to recognise any shortcomings in the referral system and to not be over-defensive of the service. It is inevitable that a proportion of clients will not end up in the right place at the first attempt, especially with multi-faceted problems involving medical or psychiatric, as well as psychological and emotional dimensions.

The Role of Supervision

In all these areas the counsellors can be considerably aided by their supervisors. They can help the supervisee to establish a number of points, including:

- whether the person will benefit from counselling
- whether the counselling needed is within the counsellor's competence
- safeguarding the counsellor's personal safety
- helping the counsellor with history-taking techniques
- pointing to evidence in clients of medical or psychiatric problems
- clarifying the nature of any medical or psychiatric problems
- avoiding setting up unrealistic aims in the counselling
- appropriate liaison with medical and mental health professionals
- the resolution of ethical dilemmas
- aiding the counsellor's professional development in these areas by suggesting reading, workshops, etc.

In turn supervisors need to ensure that they have the appropriate training and experience to lead supervisees through these areas of their work. Some other general issues to do with supervision of these aspects of counselling work are dealt with at the end of the next chapter.

Conclusion

A sound system of dealing with referrals and a professional standard of assessment are fundamental to good practice in counselling. This is particularly so for the key areas of medical and psychiatric factors and the following are important components of such good practice:

- an approach to clients that is caring, respects their autonomy and right to confidentiality, involves them in decision-making and seeks their best interests
- an adequate system for screening referrals
- appropriate liaison with referrers and involved professionals
- a relationship with medical practitioners and other staff that is professional, businesslike and respectful and seeks for co-operative solutions in the best interests of clients

- an assessment procedure that maximises the possibility of detecting existing medical and psychiatric conditions and any current treatment for them
- an ongoing awareness of the possible emergence in counselling of important medical and psychiatric issues
- working at all times with an awareness of the relevant legal and ethical issues in this area, including working within limits to competence.

4 Issues in Established Counselling and in Supervision

Issues Revealed During Counselling

Medical and psychiatric issues which predate the beginning of counselling sometimes only emerge later during the course of counselling. These may not have been revealed by the client at an earlier point for a variety of possible reasons. They may have had some anxiety or inhibition about talking about them, perhaps because they feared that they might not be accepted for counselling if their condition were known. Alternatively they may have considered their illness not to be relevant to the counselling situation. More commonly such psychiatric or medical problems occur part way through counselling, often as unwelcome intrusions to both client and counsellor that bring additional stress and anxiety for the client, disrupt regular sessions and make progress in counselling more difficult. In all these situations there will be a need to carry out a reassessment of the situation and, according to the issues involved, an ongoing process of review and adjustment.

Some clients do not reveal certain aspects of their difficulties because the questions at assessment have not been asked that would bring these to light. The assessment questions discussed in the previous chapter should help facilitate the disclosure of any relevant history. However, it is important to realise that we cannot take for granted that our understanding of the questions is shared by clients. For example, one client was asked whether he had ever been to his GP with anxiety and said that he had not. What emerged later was that he had consulted with this problem, but that the man thought that it 'did not count' because he had not been prescribed any treatment for the problem. Another client said that she suffered from depression, but when asked what the symptoms of this were said, 'It starts with this pain in my stomach'.

Asking at assessment whether the client knows of anything the counsellor has not asked about which may be helpful to know can be a useful safeguard against relevant issues remaining hidden. Assessment questionnaires, particularly CORE but also those associated with particular counselling approaches, may help bring to light medical or psychiatric issues that would otherwise remain unknown. Examples of the latter are behavioural counselling schedules, cognitive-analytic therapy (CAT) assessment forms and Lazarus' life history questionnaire (Lazarus, 1989). There will always be times, however, where the counsellor has not asked the pertinent questions, or where the client is genuinely ignorant of the implications of their medical or psychiatric history or current diagnosis.

The reassessment needed when issues emerge once regular sessions have begun may be minor in nature, leading to little or no change in the way that the counselling progresses. On the other hand, more radical change might need to be considered, such as a completely different focus for the work or postponement or termination of counselling. Where counselling has to be postponed or ended because of what has emerged, it is crucial where possible that the counselling does not stop abruptly without the opportunity for the client to resolve such areas as feelings of dependency or anxieties about abandonment.

If there has been some intentional withholding or misleading on the part of the client, the situation is more complex and needs to be approached in a different way. If a client appears to have acted deceptively it is easy to react in an angry way, but it is important to think the situation through carefully and not to respond in a punitive manner. First it is important to find out the reasons why the client has chosen to act in this particular way. The roots are often to be found in some kind of anxiety or fear, particularly that disclosure of the problem will lead to help not being offered. This may or not be a realistic fear, according to the particulars of the situation.

> When Jane came for counselling the presenting problem was her sexual difficulties with her husband. Several sessions later she revealed that she had leukaemia and feared that she would never see her young children grow up. This then became the central focus of the work and it seemed that her anxieties about her illness were too difficult to talk about until Jane had established a degree of trust in the counselling relationship. At a later point the original presenting problem, together with other issues, were also worked with and understood in terms of the effects of chronic illness and the anticipation of loss.

Dilemmas in Medical Settings

Counsellors working in medical settings face particular issues in working as part of a team or in liaising with medical colleagues. For example, the counsellor may be put under pressure to be drawn into a disagreement between the client and his practitioner about treatment of a concurrent medical or psychiatric condition in a way that she considers to be inappropriate. Where the counsellor sees it as appropriate to take up a matter with a practitioner on a client's behalf it is important to be clear that this is a response based on a sound professional judgement and not a response to a client's anxieties, distortion of the facts, or bullying of the counsellor. Discussion in supervision can be invaluable in clarifying such difficult areas.

> Jane, a practice counsellor, had been working with Alison for three months. Part of her history was of taking various medical symptoms to her GP asking for investigations which had always proved negative. Since starting counselling these kind of consultations had stopped. At one session she brought concerns to Jane about stomach pains and other symptoms which she said she was afraid would not be taken seriously by her GP, so she thought there was no point in going. Jane was concerned about the nature of these symptoms and said to Alison that she thought she should have them checked out medically. Alison responded by asking Jane whether she would have a word with the GP first.

This presented Jane with a dilemma. She felt that she did want to facilitate medical investigation of Alison's symptoms, but did not want to get drawn into acting out around Jane's previous patterns of health problems. In order to give herself time she said to Alison that she would think about this. Jane consulted her supervisor who shared her medical concerns and encouraged her to talk to the GP. They talked together about the way the conversation might be best handled. The GP responded positively to Jane's discussion of Alison's situation, with the result that Alison attended for a consultation and was referred for investigations which revealed a treatable problem.

Another kind of dilemma arises when information has been passed on as part of a referral that creates difficulties for the counsellor in making decisions about ongoing work with the client. This may arise because increasingly in medical settings people may choose to be sent all correspondence about them. An example of this is a definite or speculative diagnosis of an illness that the counsellor knows about, but that the client does not. At the extreme the counsellor may be aware that the client most likely has a limited life expectancy in a situation where, for whatever reasons, the client does not have a conscious awareness of this. In such situations there can be difficulty in understanding and responding to the material that the client brings other than in the context of the issues that cannot be mutually shared or acknowledged. There may be additional pressures if the counsellor finds it hard to live with a situation where she judges that information is being wrongly withheld or where adequate explanations have not been given. Some problems can be avoided if counsellors in medical settings are able to ensure that the referral system is set up in a way which avoids knowing certain potentially problematic knowledge about the referred person.

In some settings counsellors have the opportunity within the team in which they work to express views about the way information about patients' diagnoses is handled within the clinic or practice and where colleagues respect her views on matters such as what should be disclosed to patients. There are still a wide variety of practices, however, with some settings operating multi-disciplinary teams which work very much on a basis of equality, and others still in very hierarchical systems where doctors make most of the important decisions about the way things are done, often without consultation. Counsellors may still face in some areas a long and painstaking process of educating colleagues about the nature of their work so that medical staff understand that certain matters are fundamental to the process and that the counsellor is not being precious or unreasonable. In certain situations counsellors may need to consider making it clear that they are not prepared to withhold certain information from their clients.

Tom was referred by one of the GPs to Maya, the practice counsellor, for help with his anxiety. The counsellor was told by the GP that Tom had been treated for cancer and that his life expectancy was limited, but that he had not been told of the prognosis for his condition because he had not asked. As counselling progressed it became clear that Tom had not guessed the seriousness of his illness and this caused increasing discomfort for Maya as he was discussing important issues in a way that assumed his life expectancy was normal. This led to Maya meeting with the referring GP to discuss whether to inform such patients more fully and to emphasise the difficulties caused if counsellors are privilege to important knowledge that clients do not themselves have.

Dilemmas can also arise when a client passes on certain kinds of information to the counsellor which has not been disclosed to the referring practitioner. For example, the client may reveal that she is not taking the medication that has been prescribed for her, or even that she is misleading her practitioner about this. Through such a disclosure the counsellor can be placed in an ethical dilemma where there is a conflict between the commitment to confidentiality about client material and a responsibility towards the organisation in terms of a wider duty of care to patients.

Mohammed saw his GP because he was feeling depressed and the GP prescribed an antidepressant and also referred him to the practice counsellor. During one of the sessions he revealed to the counsellor that he was using various non-prescribed substances and that he had not told the GP about this. The counsellor was worried about how the non-prescribed drugs might interact with the prescribed medication, but also concerned not to break confidentiality as it had been difficult to gain Mohammed's trust. However, in the end she felt that Mohammed's interests were best served by discussing her concerns with the GP, but negotiated with Mohammed first and gained his permission to do this.

It is not uncommon for inappropriate pressure to be brought on counsellors to disclose any information that might be helpful to others within the practice or unit in carrying out their treatment of the client. Again education of the other professionals about the nature of the counselling contract and process is important in order to avoid conflict. They need to be enabled to understand that such a passage of information would not be in the long-term interests of their patients in general as it would eventually undermine the whole basis of trust in counselling. The question of who has access to the counsellor's records and in what circumstances also needs to be clear. These ethical problems are further discussed in Chapter 7.

There are other areas where it is important that colleagues understand certain aspects of the counselling process, such as the consequences of the regression that may occur as sessions progress. This may lead to a temporary worsening of symptoms or the client making more demands on medical colleagues. This can be further exacerbated when clients try to play fellow professionals off against each other, especially where there are divisions to be exploited. This may lead counsellors to face unpopularity with colleagues, or questioning of the effectiveness of counselling. It is helpful if a team can discuss such difficulties not only in the context of the patient's problems, but also against the background of a shared understanding of the dynamics of organisations and in particular the dynamics within the team. Clearly it is desirable to have a team that supports and backs up each other to the benefit of patients in this way, but where this ideal is not possible the counsellor will be helped in containing the situation by a clear understanding of the problem and the way that her team operates.

Non-Medical Settings

When medical or psychiatric concerns arise in the course of counselling those working in non-medical settings may feel at a serious disadvantage compared to colleagues in surgeries and hospitals. Ideally counsellors should have easy access to medical and psychiatric advice, but this may not always be possible to establish. Voluntary sector and community organisations may be able to recruit suitable professionals on to their management committees or to enlist the help of doctors sympathetic to the aims of their work. The range of the impact of the emergence of medical and psychiatric problems can be very wide, from the adding of a minor factor to the person's problems to an immediate suspension of counselling, as will happen when a client is unexpectedly hospitalised. One common situation will be where something emerges which means that the client needs to be encouraged to seek advice, probably from his GP. Organisations need to provide guidelines or protocols for their counsellor guidance in such situations, but where these are not in place counsellors will need to develop their own knowledge base and principles for practice. In certain instances the counsellor may judge it necessary to liaise with and work alongside the GP or other medical professionals on an ongoing basis, and clients' attitudes to such developments will be varied and may be unpredictable. Some who, up to that point, have showed a co-operative attitude to counselling may suddenly dig their heels in at the prospect of their GP being involved or the counsellor having contact with another professional who is treating them.

> Sue came for help with her relationship with her partner with whom she was in conflict over the demands of his work and the way they should deal together with the children. During one of the sessions she described symptoms which she thought were some kind of anxiety attack. However, the counsellor did not think these fitted the profile of the usual kind of panic or anxiety attack and suggested that she visited her GP. The result of this visit was the diagnosis of a minor heart problem for which medication was needed.

Alternatively, some clients whose attitude to the counselling process has been characterised by resistance may become unexpectedly compliant. The reasons for such reactions will only be discovered by exploring the meaning of the situation for the client, for example, that they might feel more comfortable with medicalised procedures. It is important to explore the meaning of the medical situation in relation to the counselling as well as to properly work out an appropriate course of action with the client.

In all these situations the counsellor should aim for a co-operative approach with both clients and other professionals, but must at the same time also be prepared for the possibility of confrontation and conflict with either or both. Only in extreme situations should counsellors contact someone's medical practitioner without their permission, or carry on with counselling in the face of opposition from their GP or psychiatrist. However, occasionally a counsellor may become convinced that a client's best interests will be served by these kinds of actions. Counsellors often find that these situations arouse strong feelings and therefore must be careful not to confuse acting in the client's interest with defending their professional status or responding to having their professional hackles raised.

Managing Interruptions to Regular Sessions

We have already noted that one consequence of the emergence of a medical or psychiatric issue may be the need to re-examine the viability of counselling or the appropriateness of its place in the overall treatment of the client in the new situation. This will most commonly be so when the regularity of the sessions is subject to interruptions by periods of illness or hospitalisation, unless the counsellor can accommodate such irregularities in her schedule. If it can be managed within the counsellor's work pattern, the continuation of sessions through such a difficult time can be a valuable contribution to the resolution of emotional problems. There is a risk that even the temporary halt to sessions during a period of illness or adversity can bring about a perception and experience which can make the resolution of the client's problems more intractable. During any unavoidable gaps contact by telephone or letter can be valuable, if this can be arranged. Counselling by telephone for a period may be appropriate (Rosenfield, 1997). In the case of psychiatric hospitalisation, where the value of ongoing counselling and continuity of care is usually appreciated, arrangements may be made for the client to continue the counselling or, if she is unable to leave the hospital alone, a room may be made available on the ward where sessions can take place. Some of the problems attached to seeing clients in difficult settings were discussed in the previous chapter. Exceptionally, an escort may be provided to enable the client to continue seeing the counsellor in the usual setting, but this may be subject to disruption at times when the ward is short-staffed.

During a period of hospitalisation of a significant length the question arises as to whether the counsellor should visit the client in hospital. It can feel intuitively right as a natural response and as a good way of ensuring continuity of contact. However, there are a number of possible pitfalls attached to such visits and discussion of the areas the client wants to explore may be impossible due to lack of privacy from other patients, or the difficulty of managing in a completely different and unpredictable setting. One difficulty is that the confidentiality of the relationship may be compromised in relation to family and friends who may turn up unexpectedly however carefully it has been arranged that you will be the only one there at that time. Confidentiality may also be an issue in relation to hospital staff, and the other patients with whom the client may have become friendly.

Additionally the counsellor may risk having to interact with any of the client's family or friends who may already be with the person, or who may arrive during the course of the counsellor's visit. With such people present it will be impossible for the sensitive issues that have been part of the counselling to be aired, and both the counsellor and client may struggle to find a basis to relate appropriately without the usual structure and content to their discussion. The counsellor may easily find herself part of an uncomfortable conversation consisting only of social niceties and awkward silences which later proves to have been a hindrance rather than a help when counselling is resumed in its usual setting.

Despite these difficulties there may be exceptions, and these are most likely to be in situations where the client has no family or friends, or is too far from them to receive visitors. The value of the support that may be offered in such instances may sometimes be judged to outweigh the possible disadvantages and it is helpful if the balance of probabilities can be discussed with the client beforehand and an agreement made together about what is to happen. Another area of exception is when a counsellor has been working long-term with someone with a terminal illness and she has now become too ill to attend for counselling.

It has to be accepted, though, that sometimes time pressure or lack of possible flexibility on the counsellor's part, the length of the gaps involved between sessions, the nature of the client's condition, or some combination of these may make it impossible to continue with sessions. In such instances it is important to be aware of the client's possible feelings of rejection and abandonment and accompanying frustration and anger that can be aroused by such an outcome, and to use part of any time left to look at these. One way forward may be to try to find alternative sources of help that may still be available to the client in the new situation, such as a health clinical psychologist in a hospital setting.

Glen, a student in his twenties, had not been in counselling long before cancer was diagnosed. His illness required periods of chemotherapy, during which he felt too ill to attend sessions. This was very disruptive, but as the counsellor could accommodate these gaps into his schedule, the sessions continued through this period of treatment when Glen was well enough to attend. After the end of chemotherapy, weekly sessions were re-established and Glen found these helpful in coming to terms with his illness as well as continuing to work on the original areas of difficulty.

Clients Facing Death

Where a counsellor is working with a client who is dying, this brings particular pressures. When the problems that the client brings are largely unrelated to her illness, this may bring a sense of urgency to the work, as both counsellor and client expect the time available to work on the difficulties to be limited. Whilst the probing and uncovering of deeper issues may be possible and appropriate in the early stage of terminal illness, Levy (1990) suggests that, in the later stages, the fostering of denial and other defences may be adaptive for the client where they do not hold back the client from the plans they need to make or the conversations they need to have with those close to them. It is often helpful to focus on areas which can result in an improvement or the maintenance of the person's quality of life and to help them make decisions, such as whether they wish to die at home, in hospital, or in a hospice. Lair (1996), in his book on counselling the terminally ill, suggests that death and anxiety, rather than pain, are usually the most critical issues for the dying. In her book on working with a dying client, Schaverien (2002) deals with the questions raised by this situation around the meaning of love and death.

When the counsellor works in a setting for counselling where it is common for clients to be approaching death, such as a hospice, she may find herself in a continual process of bereavement. It is strongly advisable that such counsellors' caseload should also include clients who are at a very different point in their lives and supervisors can help counsellors to be aware of this need and perhaps steer them towards additional work to provide a balance. Fisher's (1996) study looks at how professionals adjust to working in a hospice setting and concludes that it is a continuous process, rather than a developmental one with an end point. In the previous chapter reference was made to the growth in the literature on counselling in palliative care (Bayliss, 2004; Davy and Ellis, 2000).

More commonly, clients who are dying will be encountered only occasionally and bring rather a different kind of pressure on the counsellor. One impact can be that counsellors find themselves suddenly confronted with their own mortality in an unexpected way and as a result may find it hard to give full attention to the clients' material in sessions. Levy says that: 'Situations in which the therapist feels helpless to alter any final outcome, and those that confront the therapist with his or her own death, may precipitate intense reactions and have profound consequences for the therapist's own life' (1990: 209). The help and support of the supervisor can be crucial at such times as in other situations where client material arouses strong anxieties in the counsellor. Where counselling is brought to a premature end by a client's death, the sense of loss felt by the counsellor can also be usefully brought to supervision.

> Julie was referred to the practice counsellor for help with a sexual difficulty in her marriage. During the first session she mentioned that she was under treatment for cancer and Alan, the counsellor, was not sure how much this might be part of the reason for seeking help. Over the course of regular sessions Julie brought up her anxieties that her illness might be fatal and that she might not live to see her children, Mark 9 and Sophie 6, grow up. Alan experienced a high level of anxiety when talking to Julie about this area of her life, which his supervisor pointed out was probably increased by the fact that his own children were of a similar age to those of the client.

The appropriateness or otherwise of attending the funeral of a client will depend on the particular circumstances of the counselling and the wishes of the family and naturally of the client with whom hopefully there has been the opportunity to discuss the matter before their death. Where the family know about the counselling and its importance to the person they will generally be keen for the counsellor to attend. In other situations there may be ambivalence or opposition with a resultant difficulty in denying a request to attend if the counsellor makes one. Where the counsellor judges that attending the funeral is not appropriate or wise, it may compound the counsellor's difficulties in coming to terms with the death. Where the death of a client is unexpected or sudden, such as in a road traffic accident, the situation is likely to be more complex, and correspondingly making decisions is more difficult. This will be even more so if the client has committed suicide.

The Counsellor's Own Illness

A subject that arouses difficulties for counsellors is the possibility of their own illness, with attendant feelings of vulnerability, lack of control and guilt at not being available for clients. This perhaps is why it is not often discussed, and why very little has been written on it. In this account we are indebted to the review article by Counselman and Alonso (1993), principles in the BACP Ethical Framework (2002) and articles in the BACP journal. In general professional helpers are very attached to the role of being the giver, and find being the receiver very difficult. This tends to be reinforced by clients, who often like to see their counsellors as invulnerable. Additionally there is a tendency for the young to see illness as a problem of the old, as though young people do not become ill. Even so, there is also evidence that some older counsellors do not address it either and seem to become caught up in the idea that they are going to be able to carry on working for ever. As ever, prevention is better than cure, and it is important that we attend to our own well-being. The BACP Ethical Framework (2002) says that practitioners 'have a responsibility to themselves to ensure that their work does not become detrimental to their health or well-being by ensuring that the way they undertake their work is as safe as possible and that they seek appropriate professional support and services as the need arises'.

Counselling differs from virtually all other professions in the lack of the acceptability of a substitute in the absence of the usual person. An exception might be where a counsellor has a suitable colleague, and it might be useful for them to see the client in the counsellor's absence. Preferably the colleague should be familiar with the client and well-versed in the problems that might arise surrounding the leave caused by the counsellor's illness. McMahon (2000) and Rose (2004) give useful guidance on the management of breaks and emphasise the importance of counsellors talking proper holiday breaks. Martin (2001) describes the circumstances that led him to identify the need to take a six-month break from counselling and the benefit this was to him.

It is therefore important in most settings for counsellors to in general enjoy good health, to the extent that they do not regularly need to have periods away from their work with clients because of illness or incapacity. Someone considering training for long-term, particularly psychodynamic, counselling and who generally has several weeks a year off work ill or receiving medical treatment, either because of an ongoing chronic illness, or susceptibility to whatever viruses are going round, should seriously consider whether it is the right occupation to enter, or whether to adopt a different orientation. This may seem harsh and inconsistent with the currently accepted rights of the disabled, but it is important that the counsellor's rights have to be balanced with those of clients and the needs of the counselling process if it is going to be effective. Many, if not most, clients have suffered from inconsistent or absent parents and it is likely to be unhelpful, and for some clients may be insurmountable, if this is reinforced by regular and unpredictable counsellor absences. With some approaches, such as cognitive-behavioural counselling, or where short-term or non-regular sessions are offered, such considerations may not arise in the same way.

It is important, though, that people with disabilities are not excluded and course leader Linda Martin and trainee Pauline Monks (1997) give a positive account of the latter's training in counselling as a profoundly deaf person. For certain specific conditions it is possible to take action to try to manage effectively the situation with the aim of ensuring continuity at work. For example, although all counsellors need to ensure that they have suitable seating for their work, this applies particularly for those with back pain problems (McMahon and Lewis, 2001a, b).

Managing Counsellor Illness

Dale (BACP Information Sheet P9) says that there are a number of steps that need to be taken when trying to reach a decision about fitness to practise. These are risk identification, assessment, control and management, consultation and documentation. Risk identification involves considering the impact and consequences of the illness or personal crisis, in particular the likelihood that the counselling relationship will be adversely affected and how frequently this might happen. Assessment includes what strategies might enable the illness to be managed and the impact such strategies may have on the counselling relationship and contract. Particular consideration is needed where an illness may manifest itself in a particular way in a session, such as in the case of an epileptic incident. Control and management means looking at whether the risk can be eliminated or controlled. Counsellors should consult not only with their supervisors, but also with their medical practitioners, insurers and employers where appropriate. It is important to document carefully and clearly the process by which decisions are arrived at and the rationale for them. Details of consultations should also be included.

The circumstances of the counsellor's absence will have a considerable impact on the client. For example, if the counsellor is undergoing planned surgery the time when this is likely to happen can be made known to clients well in advance. A very different situation arises if the counsellor is taken ill very suddenly, or has an incapacitating accident, and as a result becoming immediately unavailable to clients for a period of time which for the moment is unknown. Counsellors working within organisations need to know what procedures are in place for informing clients and dealing with their questions in such eventualities. Those working in independent practice, or in settings where provision is not made, need to make their own arrangements. The assumption must not be made that the counsellor will be competent to deal with matters and appointing family may not be very considerate to them as they may be very distressed at the time they need to act by what is happening to the counsellor. Counsellors may like to consider whether to provide clients with information about who to contact should repeated attempts to contact the counsellor fail to bring a response.

It is not only the particular circumstances of the counsellor's indisposition that are important, but also the character of the clients' problems and the nature and stage of each counselling relationship. So, where clients have had no particular problems with life's unpredictabilities, they may be able to weather a sudden absence without too much difficulty. The crucial element is probably the impact of the event on the trust of the client, both in terms of the trust in the counsellor as a person and in the overall process. The impact of the counsellor's illness depends very much on how it is handled, either by the counsellor if the position allows this, or by those appointed to act in her stead. Illness challenges a person's defences against neediness and helplessness and makes it hard for the counsellor to give proper attention to the client's concerns about her illness (see Table 4.1 for an analysis of client concerns about counsellor illness).

Pamela, a full-time counsellor, was told by the hospital that she needed a hysterectomy. As this could be organised in a planned way rather than as an emergency, she was able to prepare her clients for an absence of six to eight weeks. A feature of this was the very different reactions she had from clients. Some became very concerned about her health and pressed her for further details about her condition. Pamela was rather shocked by one client who seemed to have no concern for her and just appeared angry at being abandoned. Discussing this in supervision made her more aware of her own vulnerability and a desire to look to her clients for concerned support in the current situation. She recognised that it was important to resist this. In supervision Pamela also identified a small group of clients who were particularly in need and would benefit from the opportunity to contact another counsellor in the organisation if the need arose during her absence.

Table 4.1   Client concerns about counsellor illness

1. Security
   Is the illness serious?
   Might the counsellor have to cancel sessions?
   Will the counsellor die?

2. Fear about damaging the counsellor
   Have I in some way caused this?
   Should I offer to discontinue the session because the
   counsellor may be in too much pain/discomfort to carry on today?
   Are my problems too much for her when she is unwell?

3. Anger
   The counsellor should not be vulnerable
   She should be strong for me
   How can he help me when he cannot sort out his own life?

In facing absences through illness or accident, counsellors must be ready to deal not only with clients' positive concern, but also with anger and other negative feelings. The latter are likely to be difficult to handle, especially if the illness has been traumatic or distressing for the counsellor. It can sometimes be hard to continue with addressing the client's concerns and not to retaliate from a place of hurt. It can also be hard where these issues persist in sessions long after the counsellor considers that things have returned to normal.

Most counsellors have days when they feel ill or very tired, but consider that they are well enough to carry on working. On such days comments can come from clients, such as 'You're looking tired today' or 'Are you ill?' When these sorts of comments are made, the temptation can be to give explanations or to ignore or deny the comments. These are not helpful responses because they generally lead the conversation to focus on the counsellor's own problems or defensiveness. Generally it is best to deal with the issue initially in terms of an exploration of the client's own concerns which might lay behind the comment, and this is especially so if the counsellor feels that she is not looking ill or tired! Where the counsellor recognises that she is probably looking below par, it is best also to address the reality of the situation in addition to referring it to relevant client material. A suitable response would be one that shows appreciation of the client's concern, but also gives reassurance about the counsellor's ability to work with the client normally in that day's session. Where the counsellor is ill with a bad cold, 'flu, or other infectious illness, a consideration over and above the counsellor's desire to work is the risk of transmitting infections to colleagues and clients, especially those who are particularly vulnerable.

The counsellor needs to judge carefully according to the situation at work and the position of clients at the time how much to make the decision himself or how much to leave clients to judge whether they wish to take the risk of catching minor illness. An important area is how counsellors look after their own needs and do not fall prey to exaggerated feelings of responsibility, distorted ideas of indispensability, or denial which lead them to continue to work when really they should be off sick. Counsellors find this area difficult and discussion in supervision about when taking time off is necessary may be needed in order to obtain a proper perspective for balanced decisions to be made.

Managing More Chronic or Serious Counsellor Illness

Where more serious or long-term illnesses are involved, the amount and kind of information disclosed will partly depend on the theoretical orientation of the work. For example, a psychodynamic counsellor working with transference may choose to withhold more than a cognitive-behavioural counsellor. All counsellors, though, need to have a flexibility based on the needs of their clients and to not work too rigidly within a theoretical stance. Where possible clients need at least to be given an idea of the anticipated length of the interruption to their sessions, or the point at which this is likely to be more precisely known.

A particular situation that counsellors in private practice may face is a reluctance on the part of colleagues to refer to them because they are suffering from a chronic illness which places limits on their ability to work normally. This may lead to tensions in relationships with colleagues or even to the decline of the counsellor's practice with consequent economic difficulties. It is better to try to have open and frank discussions with referrers about the situation rather than to avoid confrontations, even though the latter may be attractive, particularly when the counsellor is feeling ill or below par.

Sue had a condition that meant she was very susceptible to picking up infections from others which would always lead to her being unable to work for several days. The issue arose from this concerning how to deal with clients coming to her when they were likely to pass on illnesses. She decided to tell clients of the problem and make an agreement with them that they either would not attend, or alternatively arrange a telephone session, when they had symptoms of infectious illness. For some clients this worked well, but those who needed to push boundaries or act out still attended when they had colds, coughs and sore throats. Sue's supervisor encouraged her to recognise that ultimately, unless she was going to ask clients to leave sessions, she could not totally control the situation and that the best hope of changing things was to work with the material brought in the form of a challenge to part of the agreed counselling contract.

A difficult and more painful problem is the recognition that some medical and psychiatric conditions should lead counsellors to consider stopping their practice. This may be either because the person is not physically well enough to work in the way that is needed to maintain basic professional standards, or because she is not able to counsel effectively as a result of her psychological state. Counsellors need to be aware of the relevant parts of their code of ethics, particularly relating to competence (see Bond (2000) for a discussion of the ethics of counsellor's limits of competence). The question of whether the chronically ill counsellor continues to practise will be different for those who have every reason to believe they are eventually going to recover compared with those who know that the chances are that they will either remain the same or decline further. The desire to continue may lead to over-optimism or denial and it is essential that counsellors seek advice and do not refuse to act on it. At the extreme it is too much to ask clients to work with a counsellor where they are going to be over-concerned in the session in response to their immediate experience of the counsellor's health or to live with the knowledge that the counsellor is likely to die in the near future.

There are a number of dangers in the chronically ill counsellor continuing to work with clients. She may project her own feelings about her illness onto clients, is likely to withdraw emotionally from clients and may also struggle with an envy of some clients who are experienced as being 'well'. In all these kinds of difficulties it is important for supervisors to recognise and address counsellors' individual issues in this area and for counsellors to remain open to such help. One challenge for the psychodynamic counsellor is to remain neutral to clients' expressions about the counsellor's illness in the sense of not over-attending to them or ignoring them. Within many perspectives a more direct approach to the situation will be more appropriate. In any event the counsellor needs to work through with each client the meanings and implications of the illness for them. Again the extent to which this is focused on as material to progress the counselling will depend somewhat on the counsellor's theoretical orientation. Jeffries (2000) gives a valuable account of how she managed her work with clients through the diagnosis and treatment of breast cancer and the difficulties of being left with a prognosis where she was advised not to take on long-term clients.

Where denial is used as a defence by a counsellor against the seriousness of a situation, or where certain psychiatric conditions are involved, a counsellor's colleagues may have to take on the difficult task of informing or advising the counsellor who may not be aware of, or may not want to acknowledge, the growing deficits in professional ability. In any event the counsellor needs to look to trusted colleagues, supervisors and possibly his own counselling or therapy in making both professional and personal decisions in such difficult circumstances.

Whilst it may appear morbid or excessive, all counsellors need to think about what would happen in the case of their illness, indisposing accident, other unavoidable absence or sudden death and to make whatever plans are needed to ensure that professional responsibilities and clients' needs are covered. For those working in an organisation where there are other counsellors, this may simply be a matter of checking that there are clear lines of responsibility which would ensure that clients were contacted and offered suitable alternative help. Counsellors who work in more isolated work settings and single-handed private practice are advised to make a will to deal with such an eventuality, including the appointment of a suitably qualified executor. This should not only safeguard what happens to clients, but also the confidentiality of notes and other written and electronically stored materials. Advice on drawing up such a will is given by Trayner and Clarkson (1992).

Those who work in a psychodynamic way will find Haynes' (1996) account of the impact of the sudden death of her analyst of interest, and also Feinsilver's (1998) article on working with his patients after learning that he was terminally ill. Freeth (2001) movingly describes her experience of the death of her therapist who worked in the humanistic tradition and the support she received from a locum counsellor through this period. He decided to share this with the people he worked with and observed that the normal therapeutic processes were enhanced as a result of his disclosure.

Visible Disabilities and Disfigurements

If the counsellor has a visible disability or disfigurement this will raise similar, but also unique concerns alongside those discussed above. Some disabilities will arouse protective concerns in clients that make it difficult for them to experience the counsellor as robust enough to deal with their problems or able to cope with, for example, expressions of anger or issues of attractiveness and sexuality. Others may raise more fundamental concerns for clients about the counsellor's ability to counsel adequately. For example, faced with a counsellor who is blind, a client may feel that counselling will not be satisfactory because of the importance of being 'seen' and of expressions and reactions being noted visually as well as in other ways. Another example is that a noticeable facial disfigurement may make it difficult for the client to look at the counsellor.

In these circumstances it is almost inevitable that ambivalent or opposing feelings will be aroused in the client. On the one hand there is likely to be concern and sympathy for the counsellor, but on the other anger and resentment that the counsellor and the counselling are in key ways different than anticipated. It is important that counsellors find ways to become aware of the kinds of reactions that any disabilities or disfigurements are likely to arouse in clients. They then need to work out the appropriate way in which these could be responded to and managed within the theoretical framework they utilise in their work.

Inadvertent Public Disclosure of Illness

Counsellors need to be prepared for disclosure to happen unpredictably in public settings. This is particularly a risk where the counsellor lives and works in the same area and increases in smaller communities. This is a general dilemma that cannot be explored in detail here, but it is important to think about how and where disclosures of counsellors' own medical or psychiatric condition might happen. It is particularly difficult with clients who are health professionals and who might be involved in consultations or treatment with the counsellor. It is important to take into account that these difficulties apply not just to illness, but also to areas such as pregnancy and treatment for infertility.

Pregnancy

Whilst we would want to strongly resist any view of pregnancy that medicalises it or leads it to be seen as illness, there is an impact on the counsellor and the counselling which is similar in terms of preoccupation and gaps away from work. There will also be some medical involvement as a result of pregnancy, if only in terms of attendance at ante-natal appointments and classes which are likely to cut across some appointments with clients. A period of maternity leave follows a similar pattern to that of planned surgery, but with rather a different potential impact on the counselling, as we shall discuss below. Where there are complications to the counsellor's pregnancy there will be an additional impact, ranging from a degree of anxiety about the way that the pregnancy is going to a period of prolonged hospitalisation.

Additionally, some counsellors will be struggling with issues of infertility as they try to become pregnant without success as yet, with varying degrees of preoccupation with the difficulties which they are experiencing. In some cases counsellors will go on to various forms of fertility investigations and treatment which can often be stressful for both partners. Unfortunately, some counsellors' pregnancies will end in miscarriage with the consequent physical and emotional impact. Others may find themselves in the position of considering, or having, a termination of pregnancy. At the same time practitioners may find themselves counselling a client with the same or similar problems. We need to consider the effects of all these scenarios on the counselling (see Tables 4.2 and 4.3).

Disclosure

Whilst something such as the counsellor's pregnancy remains undisclosed to clients, there will not be the opportunity for its impact to be discussed within counselling. However, because such realities are not openly acknowledged does not mean that they do not have effects on the counselling. At some level the client may pick up the counsellor's excitement, preoccupation, response to feeling nauseous, or anxiety, and the pregnant counsellor needs to be aware that this may happen and be prepared to deal with it. This awareness is particularly relevant in person-centred counselling and approaches recognising the importance of unconscious material.

The point at which self-disclosure is considered inappropriate, or the pregnancy is confirmed in response to a client's guess or enquiry, will vary according to theoretical orientation. In any event, though, the counsellor needs to ensure that the client does not come to the conclusion that he is the cause of reactions to the pregnancy, or that he is wrong in his conclusions about how the counsellor is feeling. If either of these does happen, then the client comes to have a more rather than less distorted view of his perception of and impact on the world as a result of the session. The counsellor must be able to validate the client's sense of what is happening in the room without making inappropriate or premature disclosures, or risking the client feeling responsible for looking after her.

Routine Pregnancy

In the usual course of events the pregnant counsellor will be faced with the disruption of ante-natal appointments, followed by either leaving her job or a period of maternity leave as the birth approaches. Where maternity leave is taken the use of an alternative counsellor to bridge the gap might be usefully considered (McCarty et al., 1986). Routine ante-natal appointments will generally be on the same morning or afternoon of the week and so the same clients may face disruption on each occasion. Where the pregnancy is planned it may be possible for the counsellor to discover well in advance when in the week these appointments are likely to fall and for her to do a certain amount of forward planning. One decision to be made will be at what point to tell ongoing clients. This should probably be just before it becomes physically obvious, but clients may preempt this by asking before that point and the counsellor should be prepared for this. At the point of disclosure there is likely to be an immediate intensification in the relationship between the counsellor and the client. Important issues may be raised for the client at this time that there is only a limited time to work on before the counsellor takes maternity leave.

Table 4.2 Possible issues arising for clients with pregnant counsellors

Envy of the counsellor
Envy of the unborn baby
Anger, or even rage, that the counsellor has 'chosen' to prioritise care for another over the client
Anxiety about being abandoned
Identification with the unborn baby
Hurt at the counsellor's being seen as 'preferring' the baby to the client
Care about and/or love for the counsellor and the unborn baby
Linking in with own or partner's pregnancies
Feelings of envy of counsellor's partner
Triggering of sexual feelings towards counsellor
Concern about the counsellor's well-being
Possibility of a premature end to the counselling
Possibility of a gap in the counselling, the length of which may not be known until after the birth

Table 4.3 Possible issues arising for pregnant counsellors in relation to clients

Preoccupation with being pregnant
Feelings of vulnerability
Preoccupation with concern about the unborn baby
Difficulty in knowing when best to tell clients about the pregnancy
Difficulty of coping with clients' negative feelings about the pregnancy
Ambivalence about continuing to work whilst being pregnant
Uncertainty about whether to leave work or, if maternity leave is taken, at what point to return

These possibilities need to be explored and worked through without jumping to immediate conclusions about which are relevant to particular clients and which may be the most important to each individual. Clues about important areas can undoubtedly be obtained from the counsellor's understanding of her clients' problems and their story, together with the issues that have arisen in the counselling up to the point that the counsellor's pregnancy becomes a known reality to the client.

Andrea was in counselling for a number of months before her counsellor became pregnant. The counselling contract was for long-term open-ended work and therefore needed to continue beyond the counsellor's maternity leave. However, once she knew about the situation, Andrea found it very difficult to discuss the impending break in counselling, or the possibility of resuming sessions afterwards. In exploring this it became clear that she was experiencing feelings of being replaced by the baby, and was finding it hard to believe that the counsellor would ever be available for her in the same way again. Andrea was angry about the pregnancy, and about the possibility that the counsellor might have more children in the future, but found it hard to express this, the more so because she was a mother herself. The situation was further complicated by Andrea bringing various gifts of knitwear to the sessions which her mother had knitted for the baby. It emerged that Andrea did not really want to bring these and saw them as an intrusion into her counselling. The counsellor understood them as a message from Andrea's mother that she feared being seen as a bad mother and this was a way of telling the counsellor that she was a good mother.

Issues for the Supervisor

Clinical supervisors need to be able to address a wide range of issues relating to the areas covered in this chapter as they will encounter more of such issues as a result of the caseloads of their supervisees than in their own practice with clients. Therefore it is incumbent on the supervisor to have given some thought to the whole range of matters that may arise for his supervisees and to realise that counsellors' unawareness of the implications of some of the situations we have covered will be very variable. With some it may be necessary to be on the look-out for potential medical and psychiatric dilemmas and where necessary tease these out from the material that the supervisee is presenting.

A difficulty for supervisors is that they are dealing with client situations second hand, giving them less direct access to information about and from clients and also less ability to taking direct action where this is appropriate. Supervisors are very dependent on what supervisees bring and what action they may be prepared to consider in relation to their clients and so it is important to have a clear idea of the dividing line between what can and what cannot be left to a supervisee's discretion. There will be some situations where a supervisor needs to give clear advice or specific direction, and rare occasions where the supervisor may have to consider taking some responsibility to act directly on her own.

Sometimes medical and psychiatric conditions in clients create undue concern or anxiety in counsellors and supervisors at times will need to help supervisees contain their feelings rather than act on them. Counsellors sometimes need help to enable them not to take precipitous action where what they are considering is not appropriate and may even be detrimental to the counselling process. In certain situations complex ethical, or even legal, issues arise which the supervisor can assist the counsellor to resolve and these will be further discussed in Chapter 7. Whilst it is unrealistic to expect that supervisors can be authoritative sources of expertise on illness, drugs and allied matters, it is important that they are experienced and competent in the aspects of medical and psychiatric knowledge that fall within the counselling arena. This involves having knowledge of the relevant literature, keeping updated, and having access to advice from medical practitioners and mental health professionals that is reliable and readily accessible.

It is also important that counsellors who act as supervisors have regular supervision for this work. At present the responsibilities of supervisors in relation to their supervisees' clients is rather unclear, but it is evident that there is some responsibility that may extend beyond working with the supervisee if the supervisor believes that there is negligence on the part of the counsellor. It is also apparent that the supervisor does not discharge her responsibility by merely discontinuing supervision in response to a counsellor's negligence or unprofessional behaviour.

Conclusion

Counsellors must be prepared for medical and psychiatric conditions to emerge routinely with clients after regular counselling sessions have started. The counsellor needs to have this possibility in mind during sessions in order to maximise the possibility of detecting or enabling the client to reveal medical and psychiatric conditions at the earliest possible time. Some of these conditions in clients will be quite disruptive of the counselling process, because they interfere with the progress of the work or the regularity of sessions, or both, and constructive strategies are needed to deal with these eventualities.

The counsellor also needs to realise that she can become ill and needs to have in place ways of managing the impact of this on her work when it happens. In rare situations the counsellor may have to come to the difficult decision of retiring from counselling work on health grounds. Similar issues, and others, arise in the situation where a counsellor becomes pregnant. Supervisors need to be consulted about all these matters and themselves need the training and experience to help supervisees in all aspect of their work in these areas.

5 Taking Account of Medical Conditions and Their Treatment

Introduction

In Chapter 3 the issue was raised of how counsellors can make an effective assessment of a client's ongoing medical needs. Even if the client has been referred by a medical practitioner with a full list of current and previous medical problems, it is possible that at some point in the relationship the counsellor will need to consider whether they should encourage a client to see a medical team. This chapter aims to offer guidance on this issue. When we write about *symptoms*, we mean those words used by people to express unusual or uncomfortable phenomena – such as pain, excessive tiredness, dizziness or diarrhoea. *Signs* are objective physical changes, usually detected by physical examination: pallor, abnormal muscle movements, or a heart murmur. A *diagnosis* is the label given to a set of symptoms and signs based on their co-existence and confirmed with observed pathological phenomena; for example, 'diabetes' is a term for a persistently raised fasting blood sugar, which may present with a wide variety of symptoms and signs.

Most of the population is symptomatic most of the time, and psychological distress is usually accompanied by a significant increase in symptoms, so the assessment of symptoms in a client is a common challenge. The misinterpretation of symptoms resulting from painful psychosocial processes may lead to an inappropriate referral which, apart from wasting client and practitioner time, could mean that the therapeutic work is interrupted or even breaks down. On the other hand, an emerging disease condition during ongoing counselling can be missed unless both counsellor and client are willing and able to make a shared judgement on the likely significance of symptoms.

To take a specific example, a recurring headache may reflect pathological changes in the brain, or be a result of tension arising from the sense of being trapped and powerless in an unhappy relationship. In the first instance, medical referral could lead to early treatment and might even save the patient's life. In the absence of physical pathology, however, medical consultation and investigation are likely to deflect attention from important psychosocial issues. At best this may delay the counselling process, at worst it can lead to a disabling belief that symptoms are due to as-yet-undiagnosed physical pathology (Grol, 1981).

Later in this chapter we will describe a number of common symptoms which may arise either from psychosocial distress or from biophysical disease. We will offer pointers to those features of each symptom which might suggest a biophysical disease process. Good practice in effective assessment, however, requires a basic understanding that, although it may be convenient to regard an illness as primarily psychological or biophysical in origin, the majority of illnesses involve both physical and emotional factors. For example, the symptoms of migraine are caused by acute constriction of blood vessels followed by excessive dilatation. This may be triggered by powerful emotions such as anxiety or anger, and may follow an upsetting experience at home or at work. Furthermore, the decision by the migraine sufferer to treat himself, to seek medical attention, or to discuss his symptoms with a counsellor will also reflect a number of psychosocial processes. Prominent amongst these is likely to be the way in which he 'frames' his symptoms; for example, he may believe these are an unavoidable aspect of his personality, a physical disease, or a direct result of an unhappy relationship. These beliefs and attributions will be informed by his view of the world and his place within it, by the views of others in his life, and by his previous experiences of seeking medical or psychological help (Usherwood, 1990).

Thus, both psychosocial and biophysical processes may need to be considered in seeking to understand why a particular person reports particular symptoms in a particular way and at a particular time. One way of understanding the psychosocial processes is in terms of the client's health beliefs. All clients will have a set of beliefs about their symptoms which reflect cultural background, previous and recent experiences, and the views expressed by others. These beliefs will inform any fears or concerns that clients have about their symptoms, their behaviour in relation to the symptoms, and their hopes and expectations when consulting (Pendleton et al., 1984). Furthermore, these beliefs are unlikely to be fixed, but will change and evolve to incorporate the client's interpretations of their ongoing experiences and the conversations they have with significant others, including counsellors and doctors (Tuckett et al., 1985).

A second way of understanding the ways in which a person interprets, feels and behaves in relation to perceived symptoms is in terms of his unconscious processes. These are likely to be particularly significant in the context of interpersonal illness-related behaviour. Thus, the issues of why a client tells the counsellor about a particular symptom, and why he does so in a particular way, may sometimes be understood best from a psychodynamic perspective (Passmore, 1973). Other ways of understanding people's illness behaviour are in terms of 'compensation neurosis', factitious symptoms and secondary gain. These issues are discussed later in this chapter, in the section on back pain.

The best ways to assess symptoms is to encourage the client to explore these through exactly the same type of questions as are used to assess any problem presented. This basically involves starting with open questions, and encouraging the client to describe their symptoms in detail – how often they have had them before, how disruptive they are to daily function, what makes them worse or better and when they occur. Asking the client to describe an episode and the events of the day before it may shed valuable light on the triggers to the symptoms. Crucially, the eliciting of the patient's ideas, concerns and expectations of the symptoms will allow the counsellor to understand the client's perspective and to use this in further decision-making. This model of consulting also underpins effective reattribution of symptoms from a disease oriented view to a more holistic consideration. It is now widely taught to health professionals and can be applied to most presenting symptoms (Silverman et al., 1998).

However, the counsellor whose client reports a physical problem must do more than gain an accurate description of the problem and decide whether to encourage the client to seek medical advice. While evaluating the client's symptoms she should also consider and reflect on the client's associated health beliefs and possible hidden or unconscious motivations for his behaviour. The counsellor must also think about the implications of her own words and actions in relation to these factors and bear in mind that whatever she says or does is likely to affect the psychosocial aspects of the illness in some way. A shared decision-making process is better than either client or counsellor taking responsibility for this and an agreement on why such advice is given and how this should be taken forward is important (see Chapter 3). Copying any correspondence to the client for comment may avoid concern about misrepresentation of symptoms and loss of confidentiality, and may reassure the client that the counsellor is not intending to stop seeing them. Clues to a major psychosocial element being a likely underlying factor are shown in Table 5.1, and discussion of this can be used for further psychosocial exploration regardless of whether referral is actually made or not.

Table 5.1 Clues to likely psychosocial factors being a major cause of presenting symptoms

Previous symptom expression at times of stress
Tends to be introverted, does not find emotional expression easy
Symptoms are episodic, do not have a clear pattern or associated triggers
Symptoms onset or worsening often have emotional antecedents
Symptoms associated with emotional negativity, being 'avoiding' and fearful
Appears hyperaware and concerned about physical symptoms – ruminates on these
Although distressing, symptoms are without serious sequelae over a period of time (no falls or injuries)
No signs on examination except tachycardia, or possibly hyperventilation
May have a strong family or previous history of ill-health affecting coping mechanisms and resulting in learned responses to illness

Before going on to consider specific medical conditions, it is worth making another general point that almost any symptom, and many diseases, can be caused by an adverse effect of prescribed medication that is being taken for another purpose. Conversely, any medication that is prescribed for physical or psychological illness may have unintended adverse effects. A lengthy account of the adverse effects of prescribed drugs would be out of place in this book. However, the counsellor should always bear in mind the possibility of a drug effect whenever a client describes unusual symptoms, especially if a medication is new or has been increased. An up-to-date copy of the British National Formulary (also available online at bnf.org) and the ABPI Data Sheet Compendium are invaluable sources of information about intended and unintended effects of drugs. However, if there is any doubt whatsoever a doctor must be consulted.

The remainder of this chapter will be concerned largely with physical symptoms, underlying diseases, and guidance on when to refer for medical assessment. It would be impossible in a book of this length to describe every symptom and disease that a counsellor might meet in his or her career. Instead, in this chapter we have attempted to include a variety of common symptoms (arranged alphabetically), with the aim of highlighting important lessons and illustrating key issues.

We have included references in the text in order to point the reader towards more detailed and comprehensive discussions of many of these topics. At the end of the chapter there is a summary of questions that the counsellor should ask herself whenever a client discloses a new symptom or other medical problem, and we give some general advice on when to refer for medical assessment.

Back Pain

Pain in the back or neck is an extremely common symptom, and one that most people experience at some time in their lives (Humphrey, 1989). Probably the commonest variety is chronic, non-specific low back pain in which pain is felt across the lower back, in one or both buttocks, and often down the back of one or both legs. The pain may persist for months or years and tends to cause more distress than disability. The precise cause is not clear in many cases. Some people with these symptoms may have a history of back injury or an abnormality of the spine that is visible on X-ray (Jayson, 1994), although it is not always clear that such factors are causally related to the pain.

Two other varieties of low back pain are not uncommon. *Acute low back pain* may follow activity which the person is not used to, such as weight-lifting. It may also come on quite suddenly during an attempt to lift a heavy or awkward object with a bent back. The pain is often accompanied by a lot of spasm in the back muscles which may drastically limit mobility. Unless there is pre-existing chronic low back pain, acute back pain tends to get better completely within a few weeks. Another variety of low back pain which may start quite abruptly is *sciatica*. This is due to pressure on the sciatic nerve which runs down the back of the leg and commonly causes pain down the back of the leg all the way from the buttock to the heel. Sciatica is often accompanied by low back pain although the pain in the leg is usually the worse of the two. Sciatica usually improves with time although sometimes physiotherapy or an operation is needed to bring relief.

Pain may be felt in the back other than in the lower spine. The second most common area is the neck. Neck pain may be long-standing or may come on unexpectedly and suddenly. A not uncommon problem is *acute torticollis*. The person with this condition wakes with a painful stiff neck which he can hardly bear to move so that the head is held tilted to one side, often with the face looking slightly upwards. This condition usually gets better in two or three days. Pain in the middle of the back is less common and is more likely to be caused by a disease process requiring specific treatment.

There is a clear association between prolonged back pain and mood, as most pain is debilitating. Many people with long-standing back problems find that the pain gets worse when they are anxious or depressed, probably via a mechanism of tense muscles, poor posture, biochemical pain markers and central nervous system mechanisms. Occasionally treatment directed at psychological illness may bring about dramatic improvement in the physical symptom of back pain, but this does not mean that the pain was imagined or fabricated, rather that psychological adjustments have allowed other functional processes to resume more healthy patterns.

The client with long-standing neck or back pain will probably accept this as part of his or her normal experience and may not mention it to the counsellor unless specifically asked. However, a new symptom or change in symptoms may lead to discussion with the counsellor. The main purpose of medical assessment for most types of back pain is to exclude rare but treatable causes (Clinical Standards Advisory Group, 1994). Referral should be particularly considered if the client has become disabled in any way by the pain, exhibits new signs such as a limp, is losing weight, or has symptoms additional to pain in the back. Medical referral should be considered even though the doctor may not ultimately be able to offer any kind of effective treatment beyond that of diagnosis, pain relief and advice on keeping active (Waddell, 1993).

Breathlessness

Shortness of breath (SOB) refers to the subjective experience of difficulty in breathing, while the medical word 'dyspnoea' refers to the equivalent objective sign. It may be of long duration or recent onset and may be constant, slowly progressive, or 'on and off'. Some types of breathlessness are brought on by exertion, while others are unrelated to exercise or may even occur at rest. Most types of lung disease cause SOB, including asthma (which is common and episodic) and chronic obstructive pulmonary disease (which occurs in older patients, and is a diagnosis of which they are usually aware). Other biophysical causes of dyspnoea include anaemia and fluid overload, which may occur with heart failure or kidney problems; these typically cause general ill health, SOB on exertion and wakefulness at night.

Up to one-fifth of children have current or recent symptoms of asthma (Usherwood, 1987) and the disease is also common in adults. The symptoms of asthma are cough, wheeze, chest pain and dyspnoea. Symptoms usually occur in episodes, which may be brought about by triggers such as exertion, cigarette smoke or the common cold. Emotional upset may also act as a trigger in some people with asthma, but *emotional problems are not a cause of the disease itself*. Many people with asthma feel very stigmatised by their disease and pessimistic about its prognosis. These attitudes tend to be more marked in people with more severe symptoms (Sibbald *et al.*, 1988).

Breathlessness can also be a feature of psychological illness. Two particular patterns stand out. In the first the client describes a difficulty getting enough air (breathing in) such that he has occasionally to take a deep breath in order to fill the lungs properly (Gardner and Bass, 1989). He may also describe or exhibit occasional sighs as he breathes out following a particularly deep inspiration. In addition, the client may describe discomfort in the chest, usually in localised areas at the front. The pain is often short-lasting, and may be described as sharp in quality. The client may exhibit rather erratic breathing when observed. People with these symptoms are often worried about the possibility of heart disease, and may describe other symptoms of anxiety (see Chapter 6).

The second common pattern of dyspnoea associated with psychological problems is that of episodic *panic attacks*. Panic attack is defined as relatively enduring and can affect 2–3% of the population. These typically last a few minutes to an hour or two. During an attack, marked breathlessness is associated with a sense of dread or terror, often with a rapid heart beat, tight chest, shaking, light-headedness, and tingling or numbness around the mouth and in the fingers and toes. The person experiencing the attack may have a prolonged history, but may still be convinced that she is going to die. Occasionally clients with the disordered respiratory pattern and sighing respiration described in the previous paragraph may exhibit panic attacks. Panic attacks are a feature of anxiety and may also occur in depressive illness (see Chapter 6).

It is sometimes difficult to distinguish different causes of breathlessness and, if the client has not previously sought medical advice, then the counsellor and client can consider the value of this while sharing the idea that the symptoms may be due to the extra adrenaline caused by anxiety. Features needing prompt follow-up are persistent and worsening SOB, waking at night, struggling to breathe and acute severe chest pain.

Chest Pain

In addition to breathlessness, many lung and heart diseases can cause chest pain. As indicated earlier in this section, chest pain may also be felt in the absence of evidence of disease, and is usually due to muscular tension. Such pain usually occurs in one or more localised areas, and is usually associated with local tenderness. A likely cause is prolonged contraction of the muscles of the chest wall in the area of the pain. Intermittent sharp shooting pains with points on the chest wall that are tender are usually muscular in origin, while the pain of angina or a heart attack is usually described as gripping or heavy (dull/sickening) in quality, occurring in the front of the chest and spreading into the neck, back, or arms. Although it can occur at rest, an episode of angina usually starts during exertion. If the person stops what they are doing then the pain will slowly disappear. Patients with known angina are likely to have either tablets which dissolve under the tongue, or a spray which when used leads to rapid resolution of the pain.

Rarely a client with angina may develop an episode during a counselling session. If the pain does not rapidly and completely respond to the client's usual medication, or if the pain then recurs, you should not leave the client but should telephone for urgent medical advice, either from the client's general practitioner or on an emergency call-out number. If such advice is not readily available, or if the client appears distressed or ill in any way, then <u>dial 999</u>. Most UK ambulance services will send a paramedic with ECG and full resuscitation equipment to the aid of a patient with acute chest pain, which is very reassuring and allows rapid care to be put in place. They will need access to the building so a counsellor working alone should ensure that the door is unlocked on their arrival, even if this means leaving the patient for a minute or two.

Other diseases of the heart and diseases of the lungs such as asthma, cancer, pneumonia and pleurisy can cause chest pain of various descriptions. In general, it is wise to assume that a client who describes pain in the chest will need to seek medical advice. This is particularly true if the pain is of recent onset or has changed in its nature. Even if the client attributes the pain to heartburn or indigestion, they may be mistaken; it is not uncommon for a patient complaining of severe indigestion to be found to have heart problems. Conversely, it is important to be aware that clients with known heart disease are often very worried about the implications of their condition, and may experience breathlessness or chest pain as a result of their anxiety. Many such clients can benefit from acknowledgement and exploration of their fears and of the meanings which they attach to their illness, and cognitive and behavioural approaches can be useful for helping people to normalise their reactions to symptoms and resume a normal lifestyle.

Dizzy Spells and Palpitations

Unexpected conscious awareness of the beating of one's own heart is referred to as *palpitations*. The commonest cause of palpitations is anxiety, with anaemia, over-active thyroid, and heart disease being common medical causes. The palpitations of anxiety are typically experienced as rapid and regular, and are accompanied by other features of an anxiety state (see Chapter 6). Clients who describe palpitations without other features of anxiety, in whom the symptom is new, or who are above the age of thirty should be referred for medical assessment. It is particularly signif-icant if the patient has felt faint or fallen during an episode of palpitation.

As well as causing palpitations, an abnormal rhythm to the heart beat may cause dizzy spells or even loss of consciousness. Dizzy spells can result from a variety of processes, biophysical or psychological, and the decision to refer must depend upon a number of factors including the severity and duration of the symptom and the presence or absence of associated symptoms. Obviously medical assessment is needed for a client whose dizzy spells sometimes result in loss of consciousness. Such assessment will also be appropriate for a client with other signs or symptoms suggestive of biophysical disease. On the other hand, a client who gives a long history of dizzy spells along with other psychological symptoms is considerably less likely to have a medical cause.

Clients who describe a sense of spinning when dizzy will usually have a physical cause such as an ear infection. The subjective experience of rotation is known as *vertigo* and may be described either as a sense of the environment moving round the person or of the person himself rotating in some direction. If severe, the vertigo may be accompanied by nausea or vomiting. Vertigo is almost always associated with biophysical disease of the ear, brain or other part of the nervous system (Cooper, 1993) but the commonest cause is a viral infection, which may resolve in 1–2 weeks.

Fatigue

Fatigue is a universal experience following a period of mental or physical exertion, or in the absence of needed sleep. However, many people experience fatigue at other times, the commonest situation being after a period of exceptional effort, tension or demand. Emotional distress is exhausting, as anyone who has had a seriously sick relative will know. Another common medical cause is a viral illness, particularly glandular fever, or anaemia, or an under-active thyroid. Patients may have insight into the causes of their tiredness, and may already have sought medical advice. However, chronic tiredness and fatigue is also a characteristic of most mental health problems. For example, it is a key symptom of *depression,* even in the absence of sleep disturbance (see Table 6.8 in Chapter 6). The client with clear features of a depressive illness and no other symptoms to suggest biophysical disease does not need medical investigation. However, a wide range of biophysical illnesses can also give rise to the symptom of fatigue (Ridsdale *et al.*, 1993). Where this is of recent onset or without other psychological features, then the counsellor should consider referral, if only for some basic blood tests and examination.

A particular problem is that of *post-viral fatigue,* which if prolonged is known as *chronic fatigue syndrome* or *myalgic encephalitis (ME).* Fatigue during and for a few days or weeks after an episode of viral illness such as influenza or glandular fever is well known. However, in a small number of people the problem persists for months or years (Cope *et al.*, 1994). Typically the client complains of a tendency to fatigue quickly on exertion such that she is able to do far less than in the past. Furthermore the sensation of fatigue following exertion may last for the rest of the day and may persist for another day or two beyond that. If the symptoms are severe then the client may end up virtually bed-ridden, although most people with chronic fatigue syndrome remain mobile to some degree. Other symptoms typical of the related syndrome of *fibromyalgia* include pain and tenderness of the muscles (worse after exercise, with very tender 'trigger points'), joint pains, frequent sore throats and a tendency 'to catch anything that is going'. There may also be poor memory, irritability, difficulty in thinking, an inability to maintain previous levels of concentration and sleep disturbance (Holmes *et al.*, 1988). Some people develop similar symptoms without an initial virus infection (Wessely *et al.*, 1995). There is considerable uncertainty about the cause or causes of the syndrome and the various hypotheses are a matter of hot debate. The question of causality is of less practical relevance, however, than the issue of effective treatment. Although people with chronic fatigue syndrome may become depressed and exhibit typical features such as a low mood and ideas of hopelessness, the majority of people with the syndrome do not meet diagnostic criteria for depression and do not respond to antidepressant medication. Most attempts to treat chronic fatigue syndrome appear to be no more effective than allowing nature to take its course (Ho-Yen, 1990; Lawrie and Pelosi, 1994). However, Sharpe *et al.* (1996) have described a form of cognitive-behavioural therapy that does appear to be effective in reducing symptoms and improving the day-to-day functioning of people with this type of problem. The most important role for the counsellor is to allow expression of emotional distress, strengthen positive coping mechanisms, and to encourage steps towards rehabilitation. Graded exercise has been shown to be effective (Wearden *et al.*, 1998) and prolonged bed rest can be counterproductive. There are usually regional services for the most severely affected clients and these services usually have a substantial psychological component to their care approach.

Gastrointestinal Symptoms

Dyspepsia is a rather vague term which refers to discomfort arising from the oesophagus (food pipe or gullet) or stomach. Together with the mouth and throat, these two organs constitute the upper part of the gastrointestinal tract which continues with the duodenum, small bowel and large bowel and terminates at the anus. Symptoms attributable to the gastrointestinal tract are so common as to be construed as normal much of the time. Most people, for example, would not regard themselves as ill if they were to experience a short-lived episode of mild heartburn, a few hours of nausea, occasional cramping pains in the abdomen or a slight change in bowel habit. Most people would also recognise an association between gastrointestinal symptoms and their emotional state. Expressions such as 'sick with fear' and 'nervous hunger' are widely used and understood. It seems probable therefore that many clients will experience gastrointestinal symptoms whilst they are attending the counsellor and that some of these symptoms may be attributable to emotions associated with the counselling process. Much of the time, clients will either ignore these symptoms or accept them as emotional in origin.

Some people experience quite marked symptoms from their gastrointestinal tract which may be severe enough to affect their lives in some way, but which are not associated with physical evidence of disease. The commonest of these symptoms are abdominal discomfort and abnormalities of bowel habit. This combination is known as a *functional disorder*, often described as *irritable bowel syndrome*. The client may also complain of bloating or abdominal distension, though nausea and vomiting are unusual. In addition, a few people with this syndrome describe bladder problems such as frequent need to empty the bladder, or a feeling of incomplete emptying after passing urine. It is not clear whether the irritable bowel syndrome results from abnormalities of the normal pattern of contraction and relaxation of the bowel, abnormalities of sensation within the gastrointestinal tract, or abnormalities in the way these sensations are perceived and interpreted (Farthing, 1995). What is important from the counsellor's point of view is that the symptoms of irritable bowel syndrome are typically worse during periods of emotional stress and that patients with the syndrome are more likely to consult their doctor if they become depressed or anxious for some reason (Kettell *et al.*, 1992). Although the symptoms can certainly be helped by dietary modification and prescribed drugs, attention to psychological and psychosocial issues can also bring great benefit (Friedman, 1991; Guthrie *et al.*, 1993), especially if unconscious tensions can be alleviated (Read, 2005).

This section has discussed the so-called functional disorders of the gastrointestinal tract. These are conditions for which no underlying physical disease process can be identified. However, any of the symptoms described above may also result from potentially serious biophysical gastrointestinal disease. This is particularly likely in people above the age of forty when the incidence of gastrointestinal cancer starts to increase. The counsellor should consider a medical referral for any client who describes a new persisting gastrointestinal symptom, especially if this is associated with recent loss of weight or bleeding.

Headache

We have already used this symptom as an example of a problem which may indicate psychosocial distress, biophysical pathology or both. Most people experience headaches at some stage in their lives. Probably the commonest type of headache is so-called *tension headache*. This is typically described as feeling like a pressure on top of the head or a band around the head. It may be experienced for hours, days or weeks at a time and relief from analgesics such as paracetamol or aspirin may be only partial or short-lived. Tension headache is thought to arise from contraction in muscles of the forehead, back of the head, and back of the neck. It may be associated with worrying or distressing life events and may be accompanied by a low mood and other symptoms of a depressive illness (see Chapter 6). Resolution of the depression is then usually associated with alleviation of both frequency and severity of headache.

Another very common cause of headache in adults is *migraine*. This may occur at any age but usually begins between ages ten and thirty. It is less common after the age of fifty. Women suffer migraine more often than men, and over 50% of people who suffer with migraine have a family history of the same. Migraine occurs episodically, and is often of sudden onset. A period of feeling unwell, restless, with unilateral visual disturbance (jagged patterns, flashing lights), usually precede a headache, usually over one temple and eye, throbbing in nature. Nausea or vomiting may accompany the headache, and a common symptom is to find bright lights unpleasant. Untreated episodes may last for hours or days, and the sufferer may feel poorly for anything up to a few days after an attack. Migraine symptoms usually follow the same pattern in any individual, except that one-sided headaches may not always be on the same side. Sometimes triggers can be identified that start episodes in a particular person; certain foods, alcohol, caffeine, hunger, fatigue, anxiety, anger and strong emotions are common. Women may find they are more prone to migraine about the time of their periods.

A less common, but important, cause of headache is *physical trauma*. Headache following a blow to the head is not unexpected, and tenderness may occur due to bruising at the site of the blow for a week or two afterwards. However, a few people describe headache that persists for weeks, months or years following the original injury. The pain may be localised or generalised, and may vary over time in intensity, frequency and duration. It may be made worse by sudden movements of the head and by alcohol. It is often worse at times of strongly felt emotion, and may be associated with symptoms of depression such as irritability, inability to concentrate and difficulty in sleeping. The headache may be associated with feelings of dizziness or vertigo, and on occasion may mimic tension headache or migraine. This prolonged response may benefit most from counselling to explore the psychological impacts of the trauma, with simple self-help techniques and possibly physiotherapy contact for TENS treatment to reduce pain and spasm.

Headache can be a very worrying symptom and can lead to anxieties about life-threatening disease. However, serious disease is unlikely in a client who has typical symptoms of tension headache or migraine and who describes similar experiences in the past. On the other hand, medical referral should be considered if the headache is of recent onset, is becoming severe or disabling, wakes the client up at night, has other problems such as balance loss, or follows a recent head injury. Headaches accompanied by symptoms other than those described as typical of tension headache or migraine should also lead the counsellor to consider medical referral, as should a witness describing any alteration in a patient's conscious level or ability to understand what is being said.

High Blood Pressure

Systemic arterial hypertension, or *high blood pressure*, differs from the conditions discussed so far in that it rarely causes symptoms on its own. Hypertension matters because it increases the risk that a person will suffer a stroke, or will develop disease of the heart or kidneys. Treatment can reduce a person's blood pressure and in doing so will reduce the risk that he or she will suffer a stroke. It may also prevent or delay the onset of heart or kidney disease. Hypertension is diagnosed when the blood pressure is sufficiently high that there is a significant risk of developing a stroke, heart disease or kidney disease, and when the potential benefits of treatment outweigh the potential risks. Because hypertension rarely causes symptoms, the condition is often diagnosed during a physical examination for another purpose, such as an insurance medical examination, or when a patient consults the doctor about an unrelated problem.

Treatment of high blood pressure is usually by medication, although most doctors also advise regular exercise and a reduction in salt intake. An overweight patient may be advised to lose weight, and a heavy drinker to cut down, as these changes can also reduce the arterial blood pressure. The doctor should advise a smoker to stop. This will not reduce the patient's blood pressure but smoking is another factor which increases the risk of having a stroke or developing heart disease.

Many of the drugs that are used to treat hypertension cause symptoms in some people and a client may mention these to the counsellor. Symptoms induced by anti-hypertensive drugs are often vague and multi-systemic, such as fatigue, headaches, dry cough, weakness and impotence. The relationship between onset of symptoms and altered medication may help the counsellor to decide whether the cause lies in a treatment, but the client can be encouraged to discuss this with their primary care team and report back. Different anti-hypertensive drugs tend to cause different side effects so that a change in medication may help.

The diagnosis of hypertension can itself have adverse psychosocial effects, quite apart from any adverse effects of medication (Haynes *et al.*, 1978). For some people the diagnosis may be the first time that they have had to face the possibility of illness in their lives and the inevitability of death. Other people have particular health beliefs concerning high blood pressure with which they may have difficulties in coming to terms. A relative, for example, may have suffered a disabling and distressing stroke. The diagnosis of hypertension is occasionally followed by marked anxiety or depression. As indicated at the beginning of this chapter, discussion of a client's health beliefs in relation to the diagnosis, and exploration of possible unconscious processes, may be very helpful in such circumstances.

Lifestyle and the Role of the Counsellor

Lifestyle, physical health and psychosocial well-being can affect each other in a number of ways. Clients may be less able to stick to healthy lifestyles when they are psychologically unwell and the counsellor may be the first to notice any addiction or self-neglect. Both physical illness and emotional distress may be associated with changes in appetite and hence in the quantity and variety of food intake. On the other hand, too much or too little of any of the basic dietary requirements can impair physical or psychological health. This may be of particular concern with clients who are too preoccupied or symptomatic to look after themselves properly. Heavy drinkers and others whose diet lacks sources of vitamin C such as fresh fruit and vegetables occasionally develop skin and blood problems due to lack of minerals and vitamins. However, dietary deficiencies of vitamins and of most minerals are rare in the developed world, so it is unwise to attribute symptoms to such deficiency without good reason. While clients can make their own choices of supplements which are freely available in the UK, counsellors may be put in a difficult position if they recommend any supplements themselves, as supplementing the diet with vitamins or minerals without evidence of deficiency can be dangerous. They should be equally cautious if patients declare themselves as allergic to foodstuffs and additives – this is unlikely to be an issue for the counsellor, but if presented may need discussion of beliefs and concerns to consider to what extent these might influence moods.

Life-Threatening Illnesses

Two conditions which are common and where the client is almost certain to feel that their future is jeopardised are HIV/AIDS and cancer. Although there are specialist services for both these conditions, counsellors may well be seeing people who are currently well, where the illness is in remission and they are trying to come to terms both with the diagnosis and the uncertain future.

Many diseases lead ultimately to chronic illness and death. However, particular issues arise in relation to counselling people with HIV infection. A person infected with the virus may know others who are also infected, and may have lost friends or partners as a result of HIV-related diseases. They may therefore have particular expectations of the likely course of their illness, expectations which may or may not prove valid. Additionally their emotional response to their own illness may influence and be influenced by their emotional responses to the HIV-related illnesses of others. People living with HIV infection may contemplate suicide. Suicidal behaviour is especially likely following initial diagnosis and in the later stages of the illness as symptoms and disability become more severe. Other factors which may make suicide or attempted suicide more likely include depressed mood, other psychosocial problems, alcohol or substance abuse, and poor social support. In the period immediately following diagnosis adequate pre- and post-HIV test counselling are likely to be important in reducing the risk of suicide. Such counselling is normally the responsibility of the doctor who arranges the test. Pre-test counselling should address the following issues:

- assessment of the person's risk of being infected
- provision of information about the HIV virus, how it is transmitted, its effects, and its medical management
- explanation and discussion of the social and legal implications of undertaking the test and of a positive result
- assessment of the person's potential reaction to a positive test result, their coping mechanisms and social support
- discussion of issues of confidentiality.

Clients who have a life-threatening illness may have specific concerns about the implications for their family, social and work relationships. The counsellor should explore these in therapy but also encourage the patient to seek practical advice, both on financial concerns and through employers or social services. It may also be important to find supporters for other members of the family, in order that the client can continue with their own work. The profound anticipatory grief of the person with a life-threatening illness is quite different from coming to terms with the damage of the past and counsellors should ensure that they have adequate training and supervision for this kind of work. They may also benefit from becoming part of the patient's care team, and establishing the client's permission to contact other key staff as needed, particularly because symptoms in this client group may be very common and cause understandable anxiety in both client and counsellor.

Medically Unexplained Symptoms and Somatisation
(see also Chapter 6)

The Royal College of Physicians report (2003), in dealing with the psychological aspects of care, highlights the common dilemma of symptoms which though severe are not explicable with a clear diagnosis. The counsellor may be faced with clients who have had many opinions from the health service, but who feel their persisting symptoms are inadequately explained or treated. This may be a focus of anxiety for patients and may even make working on relationship issues impossible. A full reassessment as described earlier may be helpful here, but rather than suggest a further medical referral the counsellor may be better placed to seek the client's permission to discuss the situation with their doctor and perhaps even to suggest a three-way appointment so that the background to their problem can become a shared narrative. The concepts of functional problems ('it's not that there's a disease but how your body is working'), the effects of chronic tension and the links between the mind and body can often be conveyed by a trusted counsellor in a way that clients can understand and work with. If a medical opinion is needed, GPs are often better placed to reassess such issues than hospital doctors because their approach is more holistic: their clinical approach considers both the potential for disease and the many personal factors that influence what is going on with the person who is needing their help.

Tremor, Tics and Other Abnormal Movements

Tremor is defined as a rapid, rhythmically repetitive movement which tends to be consistent in pattern, amplitude and frequency (Walton, 1989). A fine, rapid tremor is a well-known sign of anxiety. However, it may also be seen in a heavy user of alcohol who has not had a drink for a few hours or days, in people who are drinking an excess of tea or coffee and in association with certain prescribed drugs. One drug that often causes fine tremor is *Lithium*, used in the treatment of bipolar affective disorder and other psychiatric conditions (see Table 6.17 in Chapter 6). Tremor is also a feature of an over-active thyroid gland (hyperthyroidism). Other symptoms and signs are *goitre* (swelling of the thyroid gland in the neck), nervousness, intolerance of heat, fatigue, increased appetite, weight loss and occasionally diarrhoea. The latter symptoms are very similar to those of *generalised anxiety disorder*, and it is not always possible to distinguish the two conditions without a blood test or other investigations. A client who describes pervasive symptoms of anxiety ought to have their thyroid blood test done if this is a new problem, especially if they have significant weight loss, palpitation, or swelling of the neck.

Benign essential tremor is rather slower and usually affects the hands, head and voice. It is less marked or absent at rest and occurs during movement, especially during actions that require fine co-ordination. A person with this condition may find that she spills an over-full cup of tea while raising it to her lips. Anxiety and fatigue make benign essential tremor worse and it tends to increase with age. It is sometimes mistakenly called senile tremor for this reason. In some people a small amount of alcohol markedly suppresses the tremor and occasionally this can lead to over-use. About 50% of people with benign essential tremor have a family history of the condition, although it may not become apparent until later in life.

Tremor occurring at rest and diminishing during movement is typical of *Parkinson's disease* (Quinn, 1995). Parkinson's disease usually starts sometime after the age of fifty, and is due to degeneration of cells in a part of the brain known as the *substantia nigra*. It gets progressively worse with time, and many people with the disease become depressed and may contemplate suicide. In the early stages of the disease it is often restricted to one hand and is sometimes described as 'pill-rolling' in nature. The tremor of Parkinson's disease is slower than the types of tremor already described, with a frequency of between three and five cycles per second. It is typically made worse by emotional tension and fatigue. Other features of Parkinson's disease are reduction in spontaneous movements (such as smiling, or arm swinging while walking), difficulty in initiating movements, and movements themselves being slow and somewhat clumsy. In the early stages of the condition, a person with Parkinson's disease is likely to be more concerned about their difficulty with movements than about the tremor. Another common complaint is of a tendency to stumble. Parkinsonism, in which the symptoms and signs of Parkinson's disease are caused by something other than degeneration of cells in the *substantia nigra*, may occur at any age. Prescribed drugs are a common cause of Parkinsonism, especially the *major tranquillisers* such as chlorpromazine and haloperidol (see Table 6.16 in Chapter 6).

Other causes of tremor are rare and are usually associated with additional signs and symptoms such that the person observing them in himself seeks medical help. *Tics*, on the other hand, are not uncommon. They often occur in isolation, may start in childhood and may never have led to a medical consultation. Tics are brief, rapid, involuntary movements that can be simple or complex; they are stereotyped and repetitive but not rhythmic. Simple tics such as eye blinking or grunting often begin as nervous mannerisms in childhood or later and may disappear spontaneously. Complex tics often resemble fragments of normal behaviour. Although tics are involuntary, they can usually be suppressed for a variable amount of time.

The main cause of tics, other than simple tics of childhood, is *Tourette's syndrome*. This is characterised by multiple tics which begin in childhood and become more complex with age. The adult with Tourette's syndrome can typically describe or demonstrate several different types of tic, and occasionally exhibits *coprolalia*. This is a compulsion to utter short, obscene words or phrases. The syndrome may be associated with compulsive behaviour or a rigid personality. In his article 'Witty ticcy Ray' Sacks (1986: 87–96) gives a memorable description of the condition, although he tends to over-romanticise it. If marked, both the tics and the *coprolalia* can be severely disabling socially. Medication can be helpful in reducing the frequency of involuntary movements and utterances. If the client has not sought medical advice, then the counsellor should consider raising this as an option.

Women's Health

The final section is concerned with a number of life experiences which are particular to women, and which may raise issues for both counsellors and their medical colleagues. There are two key hormonal conditions to which female clients may attribute their emotional and psychological problems. One is *premenstrual syndrome*, a term used to describe physical, psychological and even behavioural symptoms that are experienced during the period between ovulation and menstruation. The possible symptoms include weight gain, painful breasts, swelling of the abdomen, swollen hands and feet, headache, back ache, general aches and pains, difficulty concentrating, lethargy and irritability (Richardson, 1989). The key to diagnosis is the cyclical nature of the problem and asking clients to keep a diary of the timing of symptoms is one way which both doctors and counsellors can make the diagnosis.

The cause or causes of the premenstrual syndrome are unclear. Several theories relate to changing levels of hormones that circulate in the blood, or in certain chemicals in the brain. These theories have given rise to attempts to 'treat' the premenstrual syndrome with medication such as pyridoxine (vitamin B6) (Doll *et al.*, 1989). Although some women do report some benefit from such treatments, they rarely find that all their premenstrual symptoms are relieved. This is not surprising as there is every reason to believe that there is more to the premenstrual syndrome than changes in hormones and other chemicals. Indeed, some writers have suggested that the phenomenon is socially constructed to make women's legitimate anger a medical problem (Nicolson, 1992). Women do tend to experience physical and other changes prior to menstruation, but the ways in which they experience these changes, the labels that they give them and the causes to which they attribute them are culturally influenced. A pragmatic approach for the counsellor may be to acknowledge the reality of premenstrual symptoms described by a client and to respect her right to seek medical advice if she wishes, while not actively encouraging her to do so.

Similarly, the *menopause* is commonly associated with emotional difficulties, which include irritability, difficulty in concentrating, sleep disturbance and feelings of tiredness. Frank clinical depression may develop, and this may be a first episode or a recurrence of previous depressive illness. Although in the past such psychological problems have been attributed by some to the hormonal changes that occur during the perimenopause, hormone replacement therapy alone rarely brings much relief. It seems likely that a number of environmental and social factors are far more important in many cases. These may include children leaving home, dissatisfaction with social or work circumstances and, perhaps most important of all, unresolved difficulties in the woman's marriage or other long-term relationship. Loss of fertility, deterioration in health and awareness of ageing may also play an important part in the distress of some women at this time.

Strictly speaking, the menopause refers to a woman's last menstrual period and can thus be recognised only in retrospect. By convention, unless a woman is pregnant, or has some other reason that stops her from menstruating, then cessation of all periods for one year is taken as indicating that the last period was the menopause. **Any bleeding after this time is regarded as post-menopausal bleeding and requires medical investigation.**

The menopause usually occurs between the ages of forty-five and fifty-five, although some women experience this event earlier in their lives. The period of time preceding and following the menopause is known as the perimenopause or climacteric, and many women experience a number of symptoms during this time. Their periods may become heavy or irregular in both frequency and flow before the menopause. Many women experience hot flushes and night sweats. The flushes usually last a few minutes, although they can be longer and the woman has an unpleasant sensation of heat spreading over the face, neck and chest. This sensation may be accompanied by sweating, can occur at any time of the day or night, and may occur anything between once every few days and many times a day. Other physical symptoms that are common at the time of the menopause or afterwards are thinning of the skin and bodily hair, loss of shape and reduction in firmness of the breasts, and aches and pains in the joints (Dickson and Henriques, 1992). Later on, the lining of the vagina can become thin and dry. This may lead to discomfort or pain during and after sexual intercourse. Some women also experience impairment of bladder control with sudden urges to pass water or some degree of urinary incontinence. Most of these physical symptoms tend to improve if the woman takes hormone replacement therapy.

Couples may become less sexually active at or after the menopause. Physical changes and emotional processes both play a part, while reduced sexual activity may bring to the fore other problems within a relationship. On the other hand, some couples enjoy sex more as the possibility of pregnancy recedes. Unless the woman or her partner is sterile then conception may occur up to two years following the menopause before the age of fifty, or up to one year post-menopause after this age. Physical menopausal symptoms do not of themselves require medical assessment unless the woman feels that drug or other treatment would be useful, and again the counsellor need make little intervention in the client's choice unless she feels that the client is in need of encouragement to get help for significant symptoms.

Much has been written about the implications of *pregnancy and childbirth* for the mental health and emotional well-being of women and their families (Hunter, 1994; Walker, 1990). These are times of great change, and many pregnant women and their partners will admit to periods of anxiety associated with fantasies about problems with the baby or negative consequences of the pregnancy. An issue that may arise early in pregnancy is that of termination. This is an option which passes through the minds of many women who may wish to discuss it and to air their feelings in order to make a decision. In Britain at the time of writing termination of pregnancy is legal under the Abortion Act 1967 and subsequent amendments if two registered medical practitioners certify the need for termination under one or more of the following circumstances:

- continuance of the pregnancy would involve risk to the life of the pregnant woman greater than if the pregnancy were terminated
- termination is necessary to prevent grave permanent injury to the physical or mental health of the pregnant woman

- there is a substantial risk that if the child were born it would suffer from such physical or mental abnormalities as to be seriously handicapped
- the pregnancy has not exceeded its 24th week and that continuance of the pregnancy would involve risk, greater than if the pregnancy were terminated, of injury to the physical or mental health of the pregnant woman
- the pregnancy has not exceeded its 24th week and that continuance of the pregnancy would involve risk, greater than if the pregnancy were terminated, of injury to the physical or mental health of any existing children of the family of the pregnant woman.

There is no time limit on the first three conditions; termination under any of these is legal up to term. However, terminations after about thirteen weeks gestation become progressively more difficult to undertake and many gynaecologists will refuse to terminate a pregnancy after about sixteen weeks. A woman who decides to seek a termination will find it easier to arrange and will suffer less physical trauma the earlier she does so. A woman who has undergone termination of pregnancy may experience feelings of guilt and remorse weeks, months or years later. A potent trigger that may bring such feelings to the fore is subsequent difficulty in conceiving a wanted child. A woman's knowledge that the decision to undergo termination was ultimately her own may compound her feelings of guilt and make it doubly difficult for her to disclose these feelings. This is an area where the counsellor's own values, beliefs, previous decisions and personal experiences may significantly affect his or her ability to respond helpfully and appropriately to the client and highlights the importance of adequate training and ongoing supervision.

For those women who continue with a pregnancy, the time following delivery often brings significant emotional problems. 'Baby blues' are well known and refer to the depressed effect and feelings of misery that are very common during the first few days. Post-natal depression (see also Chapter 6) is far more serious and affects between 5 and 22% of women during the first twelve months following delivery (Richards, 1990). Many women with a history of recurrent depression become depressed during the first post-natal year but others experience their first episode during this time. Others may also have been depressed pre-natally. Two factors in particular appear to make a woman vulnerable to post-natal depression. These are a poor relationship between herself and her partner, and poor quality social support with a lack of availability of a confidant. Sadly, not all pregnancies end with the delivery of a healthy baby. Miscarriages, still-births, pre-term deliveries and abnormalities of the newborn baby all occur. Any of these outcomes may have a devastating effect on the emotional state of the woman and her partner and on their processes of family interaction. A very common feeling following an adverse outcome of pregnancy is that of guilt, often accompanied by recriminations against the self or others.

Even when the eventual outcome of the pregnancy has been a healthy child, some women feel resentment or other negative emotions as a result of their experiences during labour. The woman who has planned a home birth but ends up in hospital having her baby delivered by forceps may subsequently feel angry at herself and at others. Two factors which appear important in reducing a woman's dissatisfaction with her treatment during labour and childbirth are continuity of care by a single midwife, and the opportunity to retain choice about what is done to her. The counsellor seeing a woman before labour, particularly one who has previous mental health problems, can do useful prophylactic work to support the woman's ability to cope with the uncertainties of childbirth and early childrearing and to strengthen her coping mechanisms. Women clients who are considering conception while undertaking in-depth counselling work may appreciate advice to wait until they have dealt with their own issues before undertaking the enormous responsibility of childcare.

Chronic Illness, Disability and Pain

Many of the conditions already discussed in this chapter, such as angina, back pain or Parkinsonism may result in chronic (long-term) ill-health and disability. Other frequent causes of chronic ill-health include lung damage, heart failure, arthritis, epilepsy (Scambler, 1989), stroke and multiple sclerosis (Robinson, 1988). A number of other chronic conditions, such as arterial hypertension and diabetes (Kelleher, 1988), are not in themselves causes of disability although complications from them may be. Clients over sixty are more likely than not to have at least one medical problem, and this multiplies with each decade. The experience of developing a chronic illness has been likened to that of finding an elephant in the living room. There may be no obvious reason why the elephant has turned up in this house rather than in the house next door. The presence of the elephant is most inconvenient; explanations must be offered to friends and relatives and the whole household is affected by it. The elephant needs considerable care and attention and alters the ways in which household members act and interact, but nobody has the power to make it go away.

There is some evidence that, like many other responses to illness, individuals vary enormously in how they react to their 'elephant'. Some try to ignore it, some try to get rid of it, some adopt it and try to live normally in spite of it and some focus enormous attention on it to the detriment of other activities! Counsellors will be familiar with the idea of adaptive and maladaptive responses to adversity and are likely to see those who have had more than average difficulties in accepting ill-health. This is related to the concept in psychological studies of *secondary gain*, where disability reaps benefits such as care and attention, a cessation of difficult responsibilities, or a (partial) resolution of personal conflicts or disappointments (for example, poor self-confidence in a challenging workplace). Again, the typical history taken to formulate the problems presented will help to define the client's responses to disability, and also factors which may contribute to dysfunctional coping mechanisms sometimes learned in childhood. All these areas may present valuable metaphors for the therapeutic work.

Along with practical help such as welfare advice, nursing support, the provision of aids to living and the prescription of medication, people who develop a chronic disabling illness may need help in coming to terms with their changed circumstances. The same may also be true for their close family members. The role of the counsellor may be to help his client address the question 'Why me?' to work through any sense of injustice, and feelings of anger or shame. The client may resent the apparent good health of others (including the counsellor), may grieve what he has lost and may be anxious about the future. The reader will note close parallels between the emotional response to chronic illness and the emotional response to bereavement. The counsellor can help here by again seeking what the illness means to this client, their family and community. Different clients will have different cultural beliefs about causes and consequences of illness. The opportunity to discuss these will both be therapeutic for them and also may shed light on deeper psychological traits which will give insight for the counsellor into other areas of difficulty. It is worth noting that for some clients illness may be seen as having a significant spiritual dimension (a punishment for sin, a warning of impending death) and that counsellors may need to encourage contact with pastoral services for this aspect.

However, most healthy and healing activities are hard to undertake if the patient is in *chronic pain*. The management of pain has three components: biophysical, psychological and behavioural. Biophysical treatments include pain killers and other medication, physiotherapy, surgical interventions, acupuncture and so forth. Many people who suffer chronic pain are also helped by various psychological interventions. This is especially likely to be true if they are depressed or anxious; reduction in emotional distress is often accompanied by a reduction in the reported severity of pain. Finally, behavioural measures can be very helpful in the context of chronic pain. Advice to take appropriate exercise has long been given by doctors, physiotherapists and others. Although the rationale has often been biophysical (to mobilise stiff, painful joints for example) the benefits may also be psychosocial (increasing the patient's sense of control over his body, and promoting social interaction). More recently, interventions have been developed with an explicit theoretical basis in behavioural psychology (France and Robson, 1997).

Conclusion

In this chapter we have discussed a number of common symptoms and other problems which clients may describe during counselling. Such disclosures raise a number of issues for the counsellor. Is there an underlying biophysical disease, significant psychosocial process, or both? Why has the client disclosed this problem, in this way, at this time? What might be the implications of the problem for the counselling process and of counselling for the client's illness? How is the client coping with the problem and what are the implications of his coping behaviour? We have not attempted the impossible task of being comprehensive in addressing these questions, but have tried in this chapter and elsewhere in the book to describe common scenarios, to highlight significant issues, and to illustrate important principles.

An immediate question that the counsellor may face is that of whether or not to advise the client to seek medical advice for a newly disclosed symptom. In general, the counsellor should support clients seeking assessment for new and persisting symptoms, or a long-standing symptom becoming more severe. An experienced counsellor will be aware of those clients whose symptoms are part of their presenting problem (chronic anxiety, somatisation), and should be able to judge how much to encourage or discourage medical attention. If the counsellor does not already work in a medical setting such as a general practice, then she should consider developing a relationship with a local general practitioner or other doctor with whom she can discuss medical issues while keeping the identity of her clients' confidential.

In general, whether there is a need for medical referral or not, the client will be helped to deal with significant stressors and illness episodes if the counsellor can address the following with the patients:

- their main concerns, ideas, and patterns of symptoms
- advice about how to deal with any stressors productively; seeking personal support for practical and emotional needs, doing things they enjoy in the 'here and now', living as healthily as they can (diet, exercise, sleep)
- cognitive approaches: thinking about big issues for a limited period (rather than ruminating), practising positive thinking (what aspects of today have gone well, what have I got on my side to fight this disease ...), addressing major concerns constructively (problem solving, action planning)
- emotional approaches: normalising the need to show feelings and express negativity, encouraging expression of feelings and confiding in trustworthy others, accepting feelings of grief and anger
- psychodynamic approaches: helping the client to consider what illness means to them and how these ideas link with their childhood and social context
- explanation and reattribution: giving clear explanations as to how symptoms may be arising, how these may be made worse or better by physical and psychological responses and showing how the mind and body interact
- continuing contact with the client and their medical team, to facilitate communication.

Taking Account of Psychiatric Conditions and Their Treatment

Recognising and Responding to Serious Mental Health Problems

Most textbooks approach this topic from the viewpoint of diagnosis rather than presenting problems, but we have opted for the alternative viewpoint. For more detailed descriptions see the official guides such as the *International Classification of Diseases* (WHO, 1993) or the *American Psychiatric Association Diagnostic and Statistical Manual* (*DSM-IV*) (APA, 1994) used widely in research) or a textbook of psychopathology such as Sims (2003) or Pfeffer and Waldron (1987) from which the framework below has been adapted. Throughout the text we have indicated when medical involvement would be preferable but is not essential, when an assessment must be sought from the GP and when we feel that the Mental Health Services really should be involved either through the GP or directly. The route taken will depend on the setting in which the counsellor is working, the client preference and the accessibility of the mental health service to referral other than through the GP. If the counsellor is working in primary care it should be easier to liaise with the GP.

In many of the sections of this chapter referral is advised, but we do not apologise for this. Mental health problems require skilled assessment and treatment and clients deserve the best possible care. They also deserve an adequate explanation of why the counsellor feels that it is necessary to ask for someone else to see them. A positive rather than negative reason for involving someone else is essential and negotiation must be sensitive while recognising that in some cases clear advice may be needed. Not 'I can't cope with you' but rather 'this puzzles me ... I think it would help both of us if I asked someone else to see you .... what do you think?'

Appearance

Changes in appearance may be due to underlying physical problems, for example after mutilating surgery, or as a result of hormonal problems or medication. These problems will usually be apparent on referral and difficulty in coming to terms with changed appearance may be part of the reason for the referral. Alternatively it may be self-induced: repetitive self-mutilation is a feature of some people with severe personality problems. Very occasionally some people who damage their skin do not admit that this is self-induced but seek treatment for this (Dermatitis Artefacta).

Dissatisfaction with appearance is known as *Dysmorphophobia*. Transient feelings of unhappiness with one's appearance are common in adolescence and may also reflect a sensitive, insecure personality. Some people are undoubtedly helped by plastic surgery but most surgeons have close links with interested psychologists and psychiatrists who carry out assessments before the operation takes place. Rarely, however, a person may become totally preoccupied, sometimes in a very bizarre way, such that they lose touch with reality and become deluded and may be driven to self-mutilation. When present to this severity, this is an indication of serious mental illness, possibly schizophrenia, and urgent psychiatric assessment is essential.

Lack of care for one's appearance: Sudden deterioration of self-care can occur in a number of different illnesses, most commonly depression, but also schizophrenia and organic brain diseases such as dementia. A person with mania (described further below) sometimes adopts an uncharacteristically bright or a style of dress, which is unusual for them. This can be difficult to judge at first meeting but is clearly apparent when a longer relationship enables comparison with previous appearance or dress.

Unusual movements: Many odd movements are associated with serious mental illness, but it is not appropriate to mention the majority of them here as they tend to be very rare and most occur in very chronic psychotic illnesses for which the person is unlikely to be receiving counselling. Movement disorders are discussed in detail from a physical perspective elsewhere (see pages 65–67). A common problem, which can cause concern, is *tremor*. This is commonly due to anxiety, but it can also be caused by withdrawal from alcohol or too much caffeine. Some movements can be associated with medication and tremor is also a feature of neurological disorders such as Parkinson's disease. Drug-induced movement disorders are discussed in detail later.

Lack of movement can be an important indicator of severe psychiatric illness. In its severest form this is called *stupor*, and **urgent psychiatric referral is essential**. There is an absence of speech and movement but the person remains completely conscious. Often there is a failure to eat and drink, and this is one of the rare instances when Electroconvulsive Therapy (ECT) is used and can be life-saving. In much lesser forms depression can lead to *psychomotor retardation*, which means being both slowed down in thought and action. The retarded person looks depressed and generally delays before answering questions. They often appear much less slowed up if seen in the evening rather than the morning. Retardation is known as a biological symptom of depression and such symptoms generally respond well to drug treatment. If there is clear evidence of retardation, the GP should be involved and referral possibly then made to the mental health services (depending on severity) as antidepressant treatment must be considered.

Eating Problems

Loss of appetite and/or weight is commonly a symptom of depression. In severe depression weight loss can be marked and rapid and there may be other biological symptoms, such as sleep disturbance, loss of energy and retardation. Some people who become psychotically depressed may even have the delusion that they cannot eat because their bowels or insides have rotted away. People with other forms of psychiatric illness can also lose weight. In mania, people lose weight because their numerous plans and increasingly busy life leave them little time to eat. In schizophrenia, weight can be lost because of paranoid delusions that food is poisoned. In dementia, people may forget to buy and prepare food.

In younger people who are losing weight it is important to consider *anorexia nervosa*. A great deal has been written elsewhere about this condition (see Palmer (2000) for a clear and comprehensive psychiatric text on eating disorders; MacLeod (1981) for the sufferer's view) so we shall not dwell on it in detail here. It is primarily a condition of adolescent or young women but 10–15% of cases do occur in young males. The weight loss is usually associated with a 'morbid fear of fatness' and loss of menstrual periods. There may also be bingeing and vomiting, abuse of laxatives or diuretics and excessive exercising and clear physical signs of malnutrition. If there is clear evidence of marked loss of weight psychiatric referral should be sought although this will need to be carefully negotiated with the client. **When weight loss is severe urgent psychiatric assessment must be obtained** as in such cases hospitalisation might be needed as a life-saving measure.

Increased appetite and/or weight: Overeating may be associated with depression. Some people who are depressed are prone to 'comfort eating'. Binge eating occurs in *bulimia nervosa* where weight is generally maintained within normal limits and bingeing is subsequently followed by self-induced vomiting. Bingeing differs from 'normal' overeating because it is experienced as being 'out of control'. Many people are very secretive about their bingeing and vomiting and it is often associated with laxative abuse. It almost exclusively occurs in women.

Community surveys have revealed that milder forms of both types of eating disorder are remarkably common in the general population (see Palmer, 2000) and more than half the people with eating problems do not fit into the clear diagnostic criteria for anorexia or bulimia although they have some features of one or both and are clearly disabled by their symptoms (the so-called 'Eating Disorders Not Otherwise Specified' or 'EDNOS'; see Palmer, 2000).

Research evidence indicates that, although counselling can be effective for the underlying psychological problems in eating disorders, the abnormal eating behaviour itself tends to respond better to cognitive-behavioural therapy (see Fairburn and Harrison (2003) or Palmer (2000) for reviews of treatment approaches and also the NICE guidelines that have recently been published which are downloadable from the website (National Institute for Health and Clinical Excellence (2004a)). Family therapy is often employed with some success in younger people who are still living in contact with their families.

Feminists have written widely about eating disorders (e.g. Orbach, 2006) and a feminist perspective can be useful in understanding and helping within the counselling relationship. If progress is not being made, and the counsellor is not skilled in the specific cognitive-behavioural interventions which are clearly indicated in more complicated cases, the client should be encouraged to seek alternative help via the GP. This will usually involve a referral to clinical psychology. Effective interventions include challenging ideas about food and body image, keeping a diary of the behaviour and focusing on antecedents and consequences. A history of anorexia nervosa, alcohol abuse or deliberate self-harm tend to indicate that treatment will be more complex. Occasionally vomiting occurs without other symptoms of anorexia or bulimia. This so-called *psychogenic vomiting* can occur in severe anxiety. Rarely, this can lead to serious metabolic disturbances and requires involvement of the GP if not medical and/or psychiatric treatment.

Sleep Problems

Insomnia: Many things can cause difficulties in sleeping. Anxiety tends to cause problems in getting off to sleep whereas depression is associated with waking through the night and being unable to get back to sleep and, most markedly, with waking early in the morning. In mania the person hardly sleeps at all and so can gradually become quite exhausted. Medication can interfere with sleep in a number of ways as can physical disorders.

Sleeping too much: Some people complain of sleeping too much, feeling drowsy much of the time or of suddenly falling asleep. This can occur in certain physical disorders but common psychiatric causes can be sedatives, alcohol or depression. Drowsiness should not be confused with retardation (feeling slowed up but being perfectly awake), which has been discussed above.

Sexual Problems

During counselling, sexual problems are often disclosed. The assessment and management of these problems are the subject of many excellent books (e.g. Bancroft, 1989). Here we propose to simply discuss the presenting problems that may have serious medical or psychological relevance. Unusual sexual preferences and illegal sexual activity are often also included in a discussion of sexual disorders but these are rarely a presenting symptom of psychiatric illness.

Loss of desire may rarely have a physical cause but is most commonly associated with depression (when the onset might be quite sudden occurring in an otherwise satisfactory sexual relationship), other more long-standing personality difficulties, or problems in a relationship.

Loss of arousal in a male can have an underlying physical cause, especially the effects of certain kinds of medication. However, it also occurs in depression or anxiety and can be due to other underlying psychological factors, which may or may not be connected to a particular relationship. Impotence caused by psychological factors can be situation specific, i.e. it only occurs with a particular partner whereas early morning erections and masturbation are not affected. In women, failure of arousal is most likely to be psychological in cause but lack of lubrication can have a physical basis, for example during breastfeeding and after the menopause.

There is a growing emphasis on the medical investigation of sexual dysfunctions (see Table 6.1) and there are risks attached if counsellors assume that a problem is psychological in origin and deal with it solely from that perspective. There are a range of medical investigations for male sexual problems and the beginnings of these for female difficulties, although these are only available in specialist centres. One of the main changes in the last decade is the use of drugs to treat erectile dysfunction (see Table 6.2) and this is likely to be an important growth area in the next decade in relation to female sexual dysfunction. It is important to bear in mind that some people self-medicate with drugs obtained over the internet without adequate medical investigation or cover.

Table 6.1   Important etiological factors in sexual dysfunction

Endocrine disorders (hormonal)
Depression, anxiety, phobia, stress, fear
Drug side effects, e.g. antidepressants
Effects of surgery
Vascular diseases
Diabetes (increasingly common) and other chronic diseases
Alcohol and drug intake

Table 6.2   Main medical treatments of erectile dysfunction

Phosphodiesterase inhibitors
  – sildenafil (Viagra)
  – tadalafil (Cialis)
  – vardenafil (Levitra)
Androgen replacement therapy
Vacuum erectile devices
Rings which help retain erection

Problems with orgasm: In men, premature ejaculation is most likely to be psychological. Inability to ejaculate might be physical in origin and can be caused by drugs or neurological disturbance. Anorgasmia, or inability to experience an orgasm, is in women only rarely due to physical factors.

Pain: Except in cases where there is a clear physical cause this is commonly psychological in origin in men. In women, spasm of the muscles preventing penetration (vaginismus) is almost always psychological in origin and related to anxiety about sex. Pain on intercourse or dyspareunia, is more often physical in cause.

Premenstrual Syndrome (PMS)

The psychological symptoms of PMS include tension, irritability, depression, tiredness, sleep disturbance, mood swings and forgetfulness. Many women who complain of PMS, when they keep a diary of symptoms, are found to have symptoms throughout the month. Thus a complaint of PMS is often a more acceptable way of presenting with depression. Of particular relevance to the counselling setting is the observation that when women are depressed their mood is often markedly lower pre-menstrually. Many drug treatments have been tried but none has been demonstrated to be significantly effective for the majority of sufferers. Cognitive-behavioural therapy has been tried with some success (Blake *et al.*, 1998). A small number of women (and their partners) complain of episodes of extreme irritability and violence in the premenstrual period. There has been a great deal of publicity relating this to low hormone levels and a suggestion (not backed by research) that this extreme state can be treated with drugs. In such a situation it would be important to check for other mental health problems (including personality problems) and relationship difficulties which could be exacerbating the condition before drawing the conclusion that this is 'pure' PMS. Physical and psychosocial aspects of PMS and psychological complications of the menopause are discussed in more detail in Chapter 5.

Psychological Disturbances Associated with Pregnancy

About 10% of women develop post-natal depression in the first few weeks after the birth. These present with symptoms of depression (see page 86). A smaller number of women present with psychotic illnesses in the first two weeks after delivery. These may be depressive (about two-thirds) or schizophrenic in presentation. Health visitors play a key role in the detection of post-natal depression and in monitoring and support. Given the potential risk to the mother–child relationship if not treated quickly, evidence of post-natal depression of a severity to meet the criteria for Major Depression requires the involvement of the GP to assess what form of treatment is appropriate. Psychosocial aspects of pregnancy and childbirth are discussed in greater depth in Chapter 5.

Alcohol Problems

There are a number of factors that should raise suspicion of an alcohol problem (see Table 6.3).

Alcohol problems require expert assessment when withdrawal or 'drying out' is being considered. This is essential if there is evidence of physical dependence on

Table 6.3　Features which should raise suspicion of an alcohol problem

Physical
Increasing consultation at GP with minor illnesses
Increasing sickness absence rate from work
High accident rate (including casualty attendances)
Recurrent minor gastrointestinal symptoms (e.g. gastritis, diarrhoea)
High blood pressure
Weight gain
Morning shakes
Alcohol on breath (especially in the mornings)

Psychological
Anxiety and depression
Increased aggression
Muddled thinking; forgetfulness
Jealousy: may be risk of violence to partner

Social
Deteriorating relationships
Deteriorating standards of dress and hygiene
Employment problems
Financial problems
Driving accidents/offences

alcohol such as morning shakes or 'delirium tremens', in which the person is very confused and experiences visual hallucinations (for example see insects or small animals). It is also essential where the person has epileptic fits after stopping drinking or when the alcohol problem appears to be causing obvious mental or physical deterioration. Referral for this can be arranged via a GP or directly with a Community Alcohol Team or local voluntary agency which deals with and assesses alcohol problems. These services can also provide simple advice and information on how to cut down consumption for clients who want this form of help. Alcohol problems can benefit from counselling, and some specific approaches which can help people to successfully change their behaviour and prevent relapse can be found in Davidson *et al.* (1991). Motivational interviewing, a technique of interviewing designed to help a person to change their health-related behaviours, is increasingly used by specialist mental health workers in Community Alcohol Teams and in people working in alcohol counselling services in the initial stages of treatment for alcohol problems (see Miller and Rollnick, 1992) as well as drug problems and eating disorders.

Alcoholics Anonymous is the best-known community agency for alcohol problems. Members believe that alcoholism is a true medical disease which can only be treated by abstinence and therefore people with lesser degrees of alcohol dependence who might benefit from simply cutting down and learning how to control their drinking will not be welcomed. Nevertheless, many people get a great deal of support from AA and its sister organisations Al-Anon (for spouses) and Al-Ateen (for teenage children of drinkers) and all can be contacted via the telephone directory.

Drug Problems

Factors that should raise suspicion of a drug problem are shown in Table 6.4.

Drugs have two types of effects, those that are associated with intoxication and those associated with withdrawal (see Table 6.5).

Table 6.4 Features which should raise suspicion of a drug problem

Physical
Listlessness
Rashes
Drowsiness
Change in pupil size
Needle marks
Smell (Solvents)

Psychological
Odd behaviour
Increased aggression
Muddled thinking; forgetfulness; confusion

Social
Deteriorating relationships
Deteriorating standards of dress and hygiene
Employment problems
Financial problems

Table 6.5 Effects of commonly used drugs

Drug	Intoxication	Withdrawal
Opiates sedative analgaesic e.g. Heroin (smoked, inhaled, injected) Methadone (used in treatment) morphine, codeine tablets, *DF118* tablets, pethidine, *diconal*	Drowsiness, relaxation	Agitation, sweats small pupils constipation diarrhoea, big pupils, yawning goose flesh, stomach cramps
Cocaine stimulant Sniffed or injected 'Crack' cocaine (especially potent)	Euphoria, excitement Can cause paranoid psychosis	Mild, but profound psychological dependence develops*
Amphetamine stimulant Tablets or injection	Excitement, loss of appetite, increased energy Can cause psychosis	Depression, fatigue, headache
LSD hallucinogenic Oral	Change in perception 'Bad trips' can cause psychosis	None but 'flashbacks' occur
Cannabis milder hallucinogenic, used widely Marijuana, hash, dope. Smoked or in food/drink	Euphoria, relaxation, perceptual changes Can cause psychosis	None but psychological dependence develops*
Sedatives e.g. barbiturates (oral, injected) benzodiazepines (temazepam widely injected) *Heminevrin* (used in alcohol withdrawal but also abused)	Relaxation, slurred speech drowsiness and *heminevrin* cause death in overdose.	Anxiety, tremor Barbiturates delerium, fits
Solvents (not only abused by young people) e.g. paint, lighter fuel, glue dependence	Euphoria, drowsiness, confusion Brain, liver and kidney damage. Death by toxic effects or suffocation (plastic bags)	None but psychological dependence develops*
Ecstasy	Feelings of euphoria and well-being Depression, panic disorder psychosis can occur	None but flashbacks can occur

*Constant desire to use

There is insufficient space to do this topic full justice here, but Rassool (1998) provides an excellent introduction. Almost all areas now have specialist counselling agencies, both statutory (Community Drug Teams) and voluntary (e.g. Drugline), which can provide invaluable support and guidance. Drug agencies can also provide information about HIV prevention and needle exchange services. Possession of most of the drugs in Table 6.5 is illegal apart from some of the opiates which are used for analgaesia and solvents which can be bought over the counter. In general, counsellors should be cautious when managing people with drug problems and employ clear contracts, setting limits on what will or will not be acceptable if counselling is to continue. Specific approaches to counselling people with drug problems are also discussed by Rassool (1998). It would generally be wise to avoid taking on such clients if working entirely in independent private practice.

Odd Speech

Slowing down or speeding up: In severe depression, due to psychomotor retardation, speech can be very markedly slowed down. The opposite to this is so-called 'pressure of speech' which may occur to some degree in people who are excited or anxious but becomes very marked in psychotic illness, particularly *hypomania*. As speech become faster, reflecting faster and faster thoughts, the ideas seem to become disconnected, although in fact there are still associations between them. This occurs in *mania* and is called 'flight of ideas'. (The features of mania and hypomania are discussed further below.) It must be distinguished from over-inclusiveness, which occurs when someone talks a great deal and keeps straying from the point to tell some related story, but does eventually return to the original thread. This is usually a feature of abnormal personality (particularly obsessive-compulsive problems, which are discussed later).

In *flight of ideas* speech appears to jump rapidly from topic to topic but if you write down an example of such speech you can usually find that there are connections. It occurs in mania, usually in association with pressure of speech. If speech is very difficult to follow indeed and seems to make no sense this might possibly be *schizophrenic thought disorder* in which the person jumps from topic to topic and there are no connections and no associated pressure of speech. The first time you experience this you think that you are not somehow trying hard enough to ask the right questions and it can take a moment or two to realise that you simply haven't got a clue what the person is talking about!

Saying very little or having too much to say: In both depression and schizophrenia there may be so-called *poverty of speech*. In depression this is again related to psychomotor retardation and in schizophrenia it can be because of preoccupation with strange experiences. Having too much to say is not in itself a symptom of mental illness, but in schizophrenic thought disorder the person sometimes becomes *over-inclusive*. This is not a simple matter of digressing from the topic at hand which often occurs normally, but is much more pervasive as the person does not see that they have strayed from the point and that what they are saying is in fact irrelevant to it.

Strange Ideas

Not feeling in control of thoughts: People suffering from schizophrenia can experience the frightening feeling that they are no longer in full control of their thoughts. They may feel that their own thoughts can be experienced by other people at the same time ('I don't need to tell you what I'm thinking because you know already').

This is known as *thought broadcasting*. Related experiences are *thought insertion*, which is the experience that other people's thoughts are being placed in your mind and *thought withdrawal* where the experience is that thoughts are being removed from your mind. There is no simple checklist by which to diagnose schizophrenia, but if there is any evidence of delusions, hallucinations, incoherence or grossly disorganised behaviour, **referral to the mental health services is essential.** A number of symptoms are, however, characteristically associated with an acute onset of a schizophrenic illness and are known as *Schneider's First Rank Symptoms* (see Table 6.6) after the doctor who first described them.

Table 6.6   Schneider's First Rank Symptoms of schizophrenia

Hearing one's thoughts spoken aloud within one's head
Hearing voices commenting on one's actions
Experiences that someone or something is influencing one's body
Thought broadcasting/insertion/withdrawal
Delusional perception
Any feeling or action which is experienced as influenced by others

In **chronic** illnesses a number of other symptoms/signs may also be present:
Social isolation or withdrawal
Impairment in occupational or social functioning
Poor self-care

Psychiatrists have spent many years finding new ways of classifying *delusions*. Basically a delusion is a false belief, not shared by others of the same cultural group, which is firmly held and cannot be dispelled by argument or proof to the contrary. A delusion might coincidentally be true, but the logical basis from which the belief is derived is at fault. For example, a woman believes that her husband is having an affair and this may indeed be true, but when asked, she explains that her belief is based on his preference for a particular type of breakfast cereal! It is worth differentiating delusions from *over-valued ideas* which are deeply held personal convictions held with less conviction than delusions, sometimes understandable in terms of mood or life experiences and *ideas of reference* which occur in sensitive people who are prone to feel that people take undue notice of them or that events have a special significance for them.

Sometimes delusions arrive fully formed 'out of the blue', *sudden delusional ideas*, or they sometimes occur after a period of apparent perplexity when the person feels that something strange is going on but can't quite work out what it is, a *delusional mood*. A *delusional perception* occurs when the person attaches a delusional meaning to a normal observation and this meaning cannot be understood in terms of the person's mood. For example, a person who has felt uneasy for some days and is in no way elated in mood sees a crack in a window pane and suddenly realises that he is Jesus Christ. All these delusional experiences which do not seem to be understandable in terms of the person's underlying mood are characteristic of schizophrenia. However, other types of delusions, which are understandable, occur in both depression and mania: for example, a depressed person experiencing pain and believing that he is dying of cancer.

Most people are familiar with the idea of paranoid or persecutory delusions, but delusions can also be concerned with feeling controlled by someone else or believing that things going on around you in people's conversations or on TV refer to you (*delusions of reference*). They may also have a religious content, or be concerned with infidelity or love (believing that someone is in love with you (see below)). They can also be grandiose (believing you are special in some way), depressive (concerned with feelings of guilt, worthlessness or hopelessness), hypochondriacal (concerned with belief in bodily illness) or nihilistic (believing that parts of one's body do not exist).

A client Keith visited Henry a counsellor in private practice complaining of depression. They worked on this for a while, but then Keith stopped coming, saying that he could not leave his home. Henry agreed to visit Keith at home and he then claimed that he is being watched and that there was a campaign of psychological terror against him. Henry also learned that Keith has seen a psychiatrist and a social worker, has tried medication that appears to have no effect, and is regarded as a long-term 'case' to be managed in the community. Keith and Henry get on well and Henry is reluctant to stop seeing Keith in a supportive capacity as he wishes for this. Is this a good idea?

Comment: Yes, as long as Henry is clear and honest in his contract with Keith about what he can and cannot do to help him. His supportive relationship is clearly valued. He should encourage Keith to tell those who are involved in his care that he is seeing Henry and if there is any clear deterioration in Keith's mental state this will be particularly essential. He will not be able, within the bounds of the confidential relationship, to inform Keith's other professional carers without Keith's permission. If, however, he becomes concerned for Keith's safety he may have to reconsider his responsibilities in discussion with his own supervisor. He must ensure that he keeps full and accurate records of his contacts with Keith.

Delusions occur in all types of major psychiatric illness, i.e. schizophrenia, mania, depression and organic brain disease. Clear evidence of delusional ideas requires referral to the mental health services for assessment and it is not appropriate to go into the details of differential diagnosis here. There are, however, one or two simple rules to bear in mind if needed. In the major mood disorders (depression and mania) the delusions are usually understandable from the underlying mood (e.g. believing that you are dying if you are depressed, grandiose delusions in mania) and other features of mood disorder will be present. In schizophrenia the beliefs are not understandable in terms of the underlying mood, and other symptoms such as those described earlier may be present. In organic brain disease other features such as confusion or memory problems will be found.

Obsessions and compulsions: Obsessions can take the form of a thought, feeling or impulse which the person tries to resist and realises is clearly out of keeping with his or her own personality. These are sometimes associated with compulsions, which are acts (sometimes called 'rituals') which the person feels compelled to carry out. Obsessional thoughts can take the form of a persistent rumination which is perceived to be senseless, e.g. a mother thinking 'my child will get sick and die because I've fed her the wrong sort of baby food' even though she logically knows that this is not the case. Common compulsive acts include cleaning and hand washing because of a fear of contamination, and checking by counting things over and over again or checking door locks several times. Some people are obsessional personalities and their problems are lifelong but obsessional symptoms can become worse particularly in association with depression. Obsessional thoughts are difficult to treat but if associated with depression they often disappear as this is treated or respond to antidepressant medication. The most effective treatments in Obsessive-Compulsive Disorder (OCD) are certain types of antidepressants (SSRIs, see Appendix 2: Glossary) and Cognitive-Behavioural Therapy and behavioural treatment called Exposure and Response Prevention (ERP) and an early referral for specialist psychological assessment is recommended by NICE (NICE, 2005).

Gabby saw Bea in an agency where time limits are imposed on all clients. Bea revealed in the third session that she had some seriously compulsive behaviour, in particular checking locks and electrical appliances and wants Gabby's help with this. Gabby believes that Bea needs an experienced behaviour therapist but has difficulty finding one, and Bea anyway says she wants to continue with Gabby. What can or should Gabby do?

Comment: This depends on a number of things. How long has the compulsive behaviour been going on? What was the problem that Bea originally presented for counselling? Is there any evidence that Bea is depressed? If the behaviour is long-standing it would be entirely appropriate to spend some time clarifying with Bea exactly what her difficulties are and organising a referral through her GP to the clinical psychology services even if this takes some time. If there is any evidence of depression, particularly if the compulsive behaviour has arisen or become worse since the onset, it would be worthwhile trying to persuade Bea to see her GP for treatment. In the meantime, Gabby could work with Bea on her other presenting problems, which may be exacerbating her compulsive problem by leading to increased tension and anxiety, and provide her with appropriate support.

Body Dysmorphic Disorder (BDD) is characterised by a preoccupation with an imagined defect in one's appearance, or in the case of a slight physical anomaly, the person's concern is markedly excessive. BDD is characterised by time-consuming behaviours such as mirror gazing, comparing particular features to those of others, excessive camouflaging tactics to hide the defect, skin picking and reassurance seeking. **People with this combination of problems should be referred for specialist psychological treatment** as they do not respond to unstructured counselling.

Strange Experiences

It is important to distinguish *hallucinations* from *illusions*. Illusions occur when actual stimuli are falsely perceived; for example, misidentifying a hat stand in a dark room for a man waiting to jump. Illusions commonly occur when people are anxious or fearful. Hallucinations are perceived as being real but occur in the absence of any real external stimulus, such as: hearing voices which are not there'. Hallucinations can occur in any of the sensory modalities: hearing, sight, smell, taste or touch. Hallucinations occur in schizophrenia, depression, mania, organic brain diseases and drug-induced states.

It can be difficult to distinguish true hallucinations from other experiences such as 'out of the body' states and religious experiences (James, 1977). A general rule is that many such 'transpersonal' experiences are welcome and not perceived as frightening or alien in any way, which is not the case in most mental illnesses. An example of an exception to this would be hallucinations occurring in someone in mania who experiences 'hearing the voice of God' in a state of intense, elated mood. Therefore it is important not just to look at these experiences but other aspects of the person's condition and functioning. Transient hallucinations can, however, occur in normal experience, often when falling asleep or in the state of just waking up. These are not necessarily of any significance but any persistent hallucinations indicate the need for an assessment by the mental health services.

Changes in Mood

Mood problems are a common presenting complaint in counselling situations. Occasionally mood abnormalities can be an indicator of more serious psychiatric illness or indeed physical illness.

Depression: Depression can be caused by drugs or physical illness. This form of *secondary depression* can be difficult to distinguish from a psychological illness. Important early clues could be signs of organic mental illness such as disorientation or forgetfulness, particularly if these fluctuate. Some drugs and physical illnesses that can cause depression are listed in Table 6.7. This is not an exhaustive list and if you have a suspicion that these may be a factor, follow it up by asking about drugs and illness and if you are in any doubt at all suggest a consultation with the GP.

Table 6.7 Pharmacological and physical causes of depression

Some drugs which can cause depression
Beta blockers
Steroids and the contraceptive pill
Withdrawal from amphetamines and appetite suppressants
Ecstasy
L-Dopa (used in Parkinson's disease)
Phenytoin (used in Epilepsy)
Certain drugs used in chemotherapy for cancer

Some physical illnesses which can cause depression
Dementia
Brain tumour
Parkinson's disease
Multiple sclerosis
Influenza
Glandular fever
Vitamin deficiencies
Thyroid disease
Various forms of cancer

However, depressive symptoms will be among the most commonly encountered by the counsellor. From a psychiatric viewpoint, it is important to recognise depression of a severity to be called *major depression,* which roughly translates as 'clinical depression' (Table 6.8).

Depression may be indistinguishable from abnormal grief, which occurs when the normal grieving process after bereavement becomes blocked. Counselling strategies applicable in dealing with grief are described by Worden (2003). If there are also clear symptoms of major depression a consultation with the GP should be advised.

Table 6.8   Major depression

Presence of:	Depressed mood
And/or:	Loss of interest or pleasure
Plus at least four of:	
	Agitation or retardation (slowed up)
	Loss of energy or fatigue
	Loss of interest or pleasure or loss of libido
	Feeling of worthlessness or guilt
	Thoughts of death/suicidal thoughts
	Change in appetite or weight (increased or decreased)
	Sleep difficulties (too little or too much).
Present for at least two weeks	

There is evidence that major depression responds quickly to antidepressant medication in 50–60% of cases. This will be irrelevant if the person has a strong preference for treatment by counselling but if there is clear evidence of deterioration or a failure to respond to therapy a referral to the GP and/or mental health service should be discussed with the client. Some people who are depressed cannot make the best use of counselling interventions until they have received antidepressant medication because of their slowed and muddled thinking brought about by psychomotor retardation. Treatment with antidepressants therefore does not in any way preclude counselling and a combination of the two can be highly effective. There was a common belief in the past among therapists that being on an antidepressant would in some way interfere with the therapeutic process, but there is no evidence for this. If a person becomes severely depressed such ideological concerns should not be allowed to interfere with them getting appropriate assessment of their mood and being allowed to make an informed decision about treatment possibilities.

Sue has been seeing client Ben for counselling for a period of three months. Ben was spending a great deal of time in sessions ruminating over an affair that he had several years ago. He seemed to be having difficulty thinking clearly and sometimes appeared to lose track of what he was talking about. He is beginning to express feelings of guilt that he is apparently making little progress. Should Sue ask him to see his GP?

Comment: Yes. It seems likely that Ben is more severely depressed, and he appears to be experiencing some of the symptoms of major depression. Of concern is that his difficulty in thinking clearly, which is probably a result of the depression, is preventing him from making the best use of his counselling sessions. He would probably benefit from treatment with antidepressants which would then improve his cognitive functioning sufficiently to utilise counselling much more effectively. A combination of treatments will be optimal here.

There is evidence that person-centred counselling can be effective for depression in primary care settings (Bower *et al.*, 2003), but the evidence is strongest for Problem-Solving Therapy (Mynors-Wallis, 2005), Cognitive-Behavioural Therapy (CBT) and Inter-Personal Therapy (IPT). IPT is not well known in the UK but is more common in the USA and focuses on social functioning and relationships. The evidence for the effectiveness of psychological treatments in depression is reviewed in the NICE (National Institute for Health and Clinical Effectiveness) guidelines for depression (NICE, 2004c). This recommends a 'stepped-care' approach to depression, with treatment approach adjusted according to severity of depression (see Figure 6.1). First line treatment may involve less intensive interventions, such as guided self-management interventions using written self-help materials. Antidepressants are not effective in mild depression and NICE advises GPs to employ 'watchful waiting' before offering medication to monitor progress and intervene if symptoms do not resolve. However, many clients are given antidepressants because GPs may feel they have no alternatives to offer. NICE also recommends exercise for mild depression and this can be effective in getting a person going again. In some places it is possible for GPs to refer clients to a gym for 'exercise on prescription' for mental health problems as well as for physical problems.

Step 5: Inpatient care, crisis teams	Risk to life, severe self-neglect	Medication, combined treatments, ECT
Step 4: Mental health specialists including crisis teams	Treatment-resistant, recurrent, atypical and psychotic depression, and those at significant risk	Medication, complex psychological interventions, combined treatments
Step 3: Primary care team, primary care mental health worker	Moderate or severe depression	Medication, psychological interventions, social support
Step 2: Primary care team, primary care mental health worker	Mild depression	Watchful waiting, guided self-help, computerised CBT, exercise, brief psychological interventions
Step 1: GP, practice nurse	Recognition	Assessment

Figure 6.1   Stepped care for depression

The severity of depression can be monitored with simple rating scales filled in by the client. The best-known of these is the Beck Depression Inventory, which is very acceptable to clients and sensitive to change over time. Other scales include the Hospital Anxiety and Depression Scale (HADS) which provide measures of both depression and anxiety, and the Personal Health Questionnaire (PHQ-9 downloadable from www.impact.ucla.edu) which measures only depression. In the UK, as part of the Quality and Outcomes Framework, General Practitioners are rewarded for measuring the severity of depression in patients they diagnose with depression. In very severe depression the ideas of worthlessness become delusional and there may also be other depressive delusions and even auditory or visual hallucinations. In the presence of such symptoms **referral to the mental health services is essential**.

Serotonin Re-uptake Inhibitors (see below) are now recommended by NICE as first line antidepressants. *Tricyclic antidepressants* are now much less widely used because of their toxicity in overdose and other side effects. There are also other types of 'combined action' antidepressants which tend to be used as second line treatment for more severe depression (Venlafaxine, Mirtazepine, Duloxetine). Some people may also be taking *Lithium*, which is used either in combination with antidepressants to make them work more effectively or to prevent further episodes of depression.

If a client is clearly severely depressed but hostile to any idea of medication it is important to negotiate clearly what we are prepared and able to offer, to inform about what can be helpful in such circumstances and to try and negotiate a compromise. This might be to try counselling first but to agree that if there is any further marked deterioration the client will consider medication.

At the very least in such circumstances the client should be asked to consult the GP and the counsellor should attempt to negotiate to be kept closely informed of progress. ECT (Electro-convulsive therapy) tends now only to be used in very severe depression when the person becomes *stuporose* which means completely mute, immobile and not eating or drinking, or when there is a very severe suicidal risk and it is dangerous to wait for antidepressants to begin to work. Before the electric current is applied the person is anaesthetised and completely relaxed. They wake within a few minutes and have a brief period of memory loss and a headache. Some people, however, do complain of longer-term memory difficulties after ECT. Suicide is a major risk in the treatment of depression and the management of this risk by the counsellor will be dealt with below and in Chapter 7.

Anxiety: Anxiety is a very common symptom, which can be present to a degree in many types of problem (as well as in almost everyone). However, when severe, it is often associated with alcohol problems or tranquilliser dependence when these substances have been used in an attempt to combat the symptoms. Anxiety is very commonly associated with depression, and worry about the physical symptoms of anxiety (see Table 6.9) can lead to concern about possible physical illness (*hypochondriasis*) and subsequent unnecessary negative investigations which only lead to further preoccupation about its presence.

Table 6.9   Symptoms of anxiety

Physical symptoms of anxiety	Psychological symptoms of anxiety
Palpitations	Sense of anxiety or fear
Breathlessness	Difficulty sleeping
Chest pain	Difficulty concentrating
Headache	Irritability
Tingling sensations	Fear of impending doom
Trembling	Feelings of unreality
Tiredness and fatigue	
Sweating	
Hot flushes	
Dry mouth	
Frequency (constantly wanting to pass urine)	

Psychiatrists recognise different types of anxiety. The only relevance to the counsellor is to know that particular types of anxiety have been demonstrated to respond well to behavioural treatments. This is true for specific phobias (e.g. snake phobia, fear of spiders) and agoraphobia. Also there is evidence that panic disorder, which is episodes of panic often associated with agoraphobia and/or depression, responds to antidepressant treatment. Episodes of panic can often be helped by simple breathing exercises and distraction techniques. Generalised anxiety, which means feeling anxious most of the time, can be helped by relaxation exercises and problem-solving and here alternative therapies such as hypnotherapy and yoga techniques may help in addition to more traditional progressive muscular relaxation training which is commonly available in the form of audiotape instruction. NICE guidelines for the treatment of anxiety have been published recently (NICE, 2004c). However, just because a person is undergoing a desensitisation programme with the community psychiatric nurse for her agoraphobia, it does not mean that she would also not benefit from a counselling intervention to help her explore the underlying problems that have led to the onset of the symptoms.

Post-Traumatic Stress Disorder (PTSD see Table 6.10) is a syndrome which occurs after people have been exposed to major stressful events outside the range of usual human experience. Recent evidence suggests that it can be effectively treated but that it may be a somewhat more complex syndrome than originally thought and there is often considerable overlap with personality disorder, unresolved grief, depression, phobic anxiety, and drug or alcohol abuse. Simple 'de-briefing' involves asking exactly what happened, allowing the client to describe and relive the experience and associated emotions. It is also important to help the client to explore the meaning and significance of the event to them. The effective of early simple debriefing interventions to attempt to prevent PTSD has been questioned in recent years (Rose *et al.*, 2003) and there is some evidence that this approach can be counterproductive. Specialist cognitive-behavioural approaches to counselling in this disorder are described in Scott and Stradling (2000).

Clinical psychologists are particularly skilled in the detailed assessment and non-drug treatment of severe anxiety disorders. If anxiety is very severe the client should be encouraged to seek the GP's opinion to ensure physical causes are ruled out. Physical causes include an over-active thyroid gland, certain types of hormonal tumours and epilepsy. Specific forms of anxiety, such as panic disorder and phobias, benefit from assessment and possibly treatment by a clinical psychologist, behavioural nurse or a suitably trained CPN. Depression and anxiety commonly occur together and treatment of the underlying depression is often effective in dealing with the symptoms of anxiety. It is important to consider whether major depression is present and if so think about asking the client to see the GP.

Excitement: Over-excitement can occur in mania, but can also be caused by organic brain disease. *Mania* (see Table 6.11) often goes unrecognised and in its milder form (hypomania) can be simply mistaken for 'bad' behaviour or an irritable personality.

In mania, mood becomes elevated. When this occurs in someone who also has a history of depression it is called bipolar disorder or manic-depressive illness. The manic person often describes their mood as 'on top of the world' and 'marvellous'. At first the humour they display may have an infectious quality and it is easy to find oneself laughing along. Later, frustration about grandiose plans to 'change' the world

Table 6.10 Post-traumatic stress disorder

Experienced event outside the range of usual human experience that would be markedly distressing to almost anyone, e.g. serious threat to life, seeing another person killed.

Event is persistently re-experienced, e.g. by flashbacks, dreams. Distress when reminded of the event.

Persistent avoidance of stimuli associated with the trauma or numbing of general responsiveness.

Persistent symptoms of arousal, e.g.: sleep problems, irritability, anger, poor concentration, physical symptoms of anxiety when exposed to stimulus that reminds of the event.

May be delayed onset.

Duration of symptoms for at least one month.

Table 6.11 Mania

Presence of:	Elated or irritable mood
Plus at least three of:	Overactivity Increased talkativeness or pressure of speech *Flight of ideas* or racing thoughts Distractibility Grandiosity (including grandiose delusions) Indiscreet behaviour with poor judgement Decreased sleep
Present for at least one week (or any duration if hospitalised)	

can lead to irritability and aggression and the manic person sometimes gets into trouble with the law. Occasionally a mixture of depressive and manic symptoms are found together. This is known as a *mixed affective state*. As in depression, mania can also be caused by a variety of drugs and physical illnesses. These will not be dealt with here as it should be clear that mania of any cause does require medical investigation and treatment and any form of counselling intervention on its own will not be effective. **Referral to the mental health services for assessment is indicated and this should be arranged as urgently as possible before the situation deteriorates further**. In the acute phase, mania is treated with *major tranquillisers* (see below). In the longer term manic-depressive episodes can be prevented with *mood stabilisers*.

Mania and schizophrenia are often confused with each other and the differentiation is often not very clear-cut. Illnesses which have features of both manic depressive illness and schizophrenia are sometimes given the name *schizoaffective* and a combination of treatment is used. Excitement also occurs in other forms of psychiatric disorder, including dementia, epilepsy, schizophrenia, organic confusional states and other types of organic brain disease. Significant excitement of any form which has any features suggestive of mental illness **requires urgent assessment,** in the first instance by the GP if there are features suggestive of a physical cause.

Confusion and Forgetfulness

Confusion: Confusion can have various meanings but when psychiatrists use the word it usually means *disorientation*. This means having difficulty with remembering such things as who you are, the name of the person you are with and what time it is (time, day, date, month or year). In acute brain disease (also known as *delerium*) the person is disorientated and also has a fluctuating conscious level, drifting in and out of full awareness. This sort of 'confusion' should be distinguished from a depressed person who has difficulty thinking clearly. The more insidious difficulties related to forgetfulness are seen in chronic brain diseases and *thought disorder* and *perplexity* seen in schizophrenia and mania. The presence of 'confusion' indicates that **medical investigation is required urgently** as many disorders which present with a picture of acute organic brain disease can be reversible if treated quickly and may also be life threatening, such as drug intoxications, alcohol withdrawal, infections such as encephalitis or meningitis and cardiovascular disease.

Forgetfulness: Many people complain of forgetfulness. When people are very anxious they sometimes seem forgetful but on testing it is clear the problem is that their concentration is so impaired that they have difficulty attending to and registering new memories. In depression, memory sometimes seems impaired for a similar reason and also because thinking is slowed up. More severe memory impairment is seen in chronic organic brain diseases, such as *dementia*, where the forgetfulness is usually associated with other features such as impaired intellectual performance and disorientation. People who have experienced head injuries may have long-lasting memory problems. Alcohol abuse is another common cause of this problem.

Physical Symptoms

It is not unusual for psychiatric illness to present with physical symptoms. Clearly if a client is presenting new and worrying physical symptoms to you it will be necessary to encourage them to seek medical advice. However, it is important to mention here the situations in which physical symptoms do not denote an underlying physical disorder as the counsellor may become involved in the care of a person in which physical symptoms are a presenting feature of underlying psychological distress. This phenomenon is known by a variety of names. The most commonly used terms are *somatisation*, which suggests a process by which emotional symptoms are 'converted' into somatic symptoms, Functional Somatic Symptoms and Medically Unexplained Symptoms. This kind of problem is very commonly seen by GPs (Gask, 1995). Many people are unhappy about talking about emotional problems to doctors for a number of reasons, one of the most important of which is the stigma of mental illness. Because of this, sometimes people go to the doctor to complain about the physical symptoms that accompany emotional illness, such as palpitations caused by anxiety or weight loss caused by depression. People can become preoccupied with the worry or fear that they have a serious physical illness (known as *hypochondriasis*). If their depression or anxiety is missed, and the symptoms investigated, this can further convince the person that they do have an underlying physical disorder. When the GP tries to help the patient to accept a psychological view of their problems it may then be more difficult than it might have been earlier. A useful practical model for managing somatisation in primary care, called 'Reattribution' (see Table 6.12) which is of help to both GPs and counsellors is described in Goldberg *et al.*, 1989; see also the video version by Gask *et al.*, 2002. This approach deals with engaging people in talking about emotional as well as physical symptoms and helping them to make links between the two.

Table 6.12 The 'Reattribution' model for managing people who have medically unexplained symptoms

Stage 1: Feeling understood
Take history of presenting physical symptoms, other associated physical symptoms, emotional symptoms and psychosocial factors, symptom beliefs, past similar symptoms and management, brief focused physical examination.

Stage 2: Broadening the agenda
Feed back results of physical examination and any investigations (including no or minor abnormalities), explains implications of findings, i.e. lack of serious underlying pathology, acknowledgement of patient's presenting symptoms with associated, distress and impairment of function, explores possibility that physical symptoms might be linked to psychosocial factors.

Stage 3: Making the link
Link the physical symptom to an underlying psychosocial or lifestyle issue using a normalising physiological, temporal or social link. Examples: 'stress at home causes muscles in your body such as your back to tense and muscles held tight for long periods ache', 'back ache occurs each time you row with your partner', 'talking about your problems now have brought on your back pain', 'frustration about not working leads to depression and depression lowers the pain threshold and makes you tired', 'when your parents rowed at home your mother went to bed complaining of a headache and now each time you have a row you get a headache'.

Stage 4: Negotiating further treatment
No further follow-up or treatment required, further review of symptoms and psychosocial factors over time to test or refine explanation, symptomatic treatment or treatment of underlying psychosocial or lifestyle issues.

The counsellor could become involved in this problem area particularly when working in a medical setting where the GP refers the patient. It may take some time to engage such a client in talking about emotions and good liaison with the GP is essential to discuss how to respond to physical complaints and the terms of the GP's continuing role and responsibility for examination and investigations. It is important to try to avoid adopting a stance whereby, for example, a counsellor working in a medical setting might get into conflict with the GP about whether further investigations or treatment are necessary. Such a scenario would possibly suggest some over-identification which should be explored in supervision. The most difficult area will lie around illnesses such as ME about which doctors disagree with each other. However, even if the counsellor believes that the client is not getting the right treatment he or she should try to avoid stepping into the role of advising further interventions and especially not act as the client's advocate with their GP. A problem occurs if the counsellor is employed in an agency where he is also expected to act in an advocacy role. The problems inherent in combining these roles are discussed in Chapter 7.

Violent Behaviour

Violent behaviour is not uncommonly associated with personality disorder, where there is likely to be a long history of similar events. Violent incidents sometimes occur when people are under the influence of alcohol and drugs and this may also be associated with personality disorder. Where violence is threatened towards partners or spouses there is often evidence of morbid jealousy (see below).

Depression can be associated with violence, not only with suicide but also with homicidal acts, often against the person's family followed by suicide. **Threats must be taken seriously** and this is a situation where absolute confidentiality should be questioned. In mania violence may erupt when an irritable manic person is thwarted. Finally, violent episodes do also occur in people with schizophrenia but are uncommon. They are often unprovoked and may seem senseless to someone with no knowledge of the person's inner world. In the context of counselling, if a relative who is being counselled reports episodes of hostility and irritability and feels afraid, their fears should be taken seriously. There is insufficient space here to discuss all the ways in which transgressions against the law (common examples which a counsellor might come into contact with are shoplifting and criminal damage) can indicate the presence of psychiatric illness. **Where there is any threat of violence the assessment of the mental health service must be sought unless the counsellor is <u>absolutely clear</u> there is no evidence of mental illness.**

Some Special Topics

Responding to Suicidal Ideas

The ethical and legal issues involved in dealing with a client's suicidal ideas have been addressed elsewhere in this book (see Chapter 7). From a psychiatric point of view, suicide is seen as essentially preventable if the person is suffering from a treatable mental illness such that the suicidal ideation would no longer be expressed if the person received and responded to treatment adequately. The majority of people who successfully complete suicide are suffering from depression (around 70–80%), a smaller proportion (about 15%) from alcohol dependence and the remainder is made up by those with schizophrenic illnesses, personality disorders, drug misuse and finally no psychiatric disorder. In the past the majority of people who committed suicide had contact with their GP in the month before the suicide, but this is no longer the case and the largest 'growth area' is now in young men who have much less contact with statutory agencies and tend to be less likely to be 'clinically' depressed. It is for the individual practitioner to decide, in consultation with the supervisor, when to respect the wishes of a client who does not want any (usually further) psychiatric intervention. If there is, however, suggestion that psychiatric intervention might avert suicide such that, when treated, the client would feel differently about ending his life, the question of such an intervention must be debated with the client, if not by the counsellor then by the GP or mental health professional.

A small number of people each year commit murder and then kill themselves. In some of these cases the person is depressed and believes that the world is an unsafe place, for example, for their child, as in the case of a depressed mother who kills her child. However, some cases are men who have been separated from their children through divorce and kill their children rather than allow their spouse to keep them, and others are morbidly jealous (see below). **All threats made about others should be taken seriously.** This is an occasion when the confidentiality of the client–therapist relationship should be reviewed.

Jealousy, Erotomania and Stalking

Morbid jealousy can be identified when jealousy dominates a partner's every thought and action. Morbidly jealous men follow their partners around and cannot be reassured that there is not a problem. They may check their partner's underwear for stains, misinterpret events as indicators of unfaithfulness and put unreasonable constraints on their partners which cause great distress. It is often associated with alcoholism but can also occur in other forms of psychiatric illness, such as depression and schizophrenia, and in personality disorder (see below). If identified, the safety of the spouse is paramount as it can be a cause of serious and often homicidal domestic violence. **If specific threats are made against the object of jealousy this is an instance when the confidentiality of the therapist–client relationship should be reviewed and appropriate action taken**.

Erotomania (also known as De Clerambault's syndrome): Some people claim that another person (often of higher social status and sometimes a celebrity) is in love with them, to the intensity of this being a delusion, even though there is no good evidence that this is the case. Some begin to harass the other person, but physical harm is very unusual. This problem, which formed the subject of Ian McEwan's novel *Enduring Love*, can occur in many different psychiatric illnesses including a pure form 'primary erotomania' where the delusion of love is the only apparent symptom, and is not easy to treat even with medication.

Stalking: Stalking is a behaviour typically involving the intrusive following of a 'target', for instance standing in front of the target's home or other unexpected intrusions in their private domain. Stalkers most often persecute their targets by unwanted communications which can consist of frequent (often nightly) telephone calls, letters, e-mail, graffiti, notes or packages. Extreme forms include ordering goods in the person's name, threatening the victim with violence or actually attacking them. In some cases the stalker goes on to commit murder. Stalkers may be psychotic, for example with primary erotomania, schizophrenia, depression or bipolar disorder, or have a personality disorder. Counsellors and psychotherapists have been stalked by ex-clients and it is important to be able as far as possible to minimise the risk of this. Where there is any evidence of developing abnormal behaviour this should be appropriately responded to before any subsequent resentment spilling over into stalking behaviour. For more detail see Kamphuis and Emmelkamp (2000) and also see Chapter 7.

Personality Disorder

Personality disorders are difficult to define and it is not easy to decide where normal personality changes into a personality problem and this then becomes serious enough to be labelled as a personality disorder. The World Health Organisation defines personality disorders as:

> Deeply ingrained and enduring behaviour patterns manifesting themselves as inflexible responses to a broad range of personal and social situations. They represent either extreme or significant deviations from the way the average

individual in a given culture perceives, thinks, feels and particularly relates to others. Such behaviour patterns tend to be stable and become multiple domains of behaviour and social functioning. They are frequently, but not always, associated with various degrees of subjective distress and problems in social functioning and social performance (WHO, 1993).

Personality tends to be stable over time and disorders are usually recognisable in adolescence or early adult life and persist into middle age, when they generally seem to become less obvious. However, this is not always the case, as people who work with the elderly will recognise. Psychiatrists have spent many years inventing (and failing to agree on) categorical labels for abnormal personalities but people rarely fit one exactly, and these labels should be used with some caution. A typology of the more commonly used terms can be found in Table 6.13.

In practice most people, normal or abnormal, possess a number of different personality traits rather than easily fitting into one category, and there are probably many more varieties of abnormal personality than the classical 'types' described below. Some use the term 'character disorder' to describe a constellation of personality traits which may cause conscious distress to clients and those close to them but which does not warrant the frankly more pejorative term 'personality disorder'.

Table 6.13   A typology of personality disorders

Affective	Lifelong abnormality of mood which may be depressive, elated, changing from one to the other (cyclothymic).
Anti-social	Commonly called 'psychopaths' or 'sociopaths'. Anti-social behaviour with absence of conscience, inability to learn from mistakes, and a long history of disturbance and often violence problems with the law. Often described as superficially very charming and 'plausible'.
Avoidant	Also called anxious. Hypersensitive, timid, self-conscious.
Borderline	Instability of mood, interpersonal relationships and self-imaging.
Dependent	Inability to cope with normal demands. Submissive, helpless.
Depressive	Lifelong depressive temperament (can be confused with or co-exist with depressive illness).
Explosive	Uncontrollable outbursts of aggression, physical or verbal but not otherwise anti-social.
Histrionic	Sometimes called 'hysterical'. Demanding and attention-seeking, emotionally shallow, dramatic, egocentric (often an abusive label applied without due grounds to difficult female patients by male doctors).
Narcissistic	Grandiose, self-important, hypersensitive to the evaluation of others.
Obsessional	Rigid, compulsive, inflexible and perfectionist. Also called 'anankastic'.
Paranoid	Sensitive, suspicious and may be jealous. Often litigious.
Passive/Aggressive	Passive resistance to demands for adequate social and occupational performance. Sulky, resentful, avoids obligations.
Schizoid	Withdrawn, introspective and detached. Indifference to social relationships. Restricted range of emotional experience and expression.
Schizotypal	Isolated, eccentric ideas.

The presence of a personality disorder does not preclude the additional development of mental illness. Alternatively some clients may demonstrate some of the features of a personality disorder when they have in fact developed a mental illness although no such signs were apparent before the onset of the illness.

Clients with features of Borderline Personality Disorder (see Table 6.14) may be particularly challenging and their problems may not always become apparent until a therapeutic contract has commenced. Clients may superficially cope well in day-to-day life but later begin to disintegrate more overtly. They have unstable relationships with others, often of an intense, short-term nature, impulsive behaviour, and suffer brief periods of depression associated with suicidal behaviour. Many of these people also abuse alcohol and drugs and some also experience brief episodes in which they do lose touch with reality and experience psychotic symptoms. These people cause a great deal of anxiety in both general practice and psychiatric settings, but are often deemed unsuitable for formal insight-oriented psychotherapy or counselling. They seem to respond better to a more limited supportive commitment over a long period of time although recent work has suggested that Cognitive Analytic Therapy (CAT) may be helpful (Ryle, 1997).

Table 6.14   Criteria for Borderline Personality Disorder

Five or more of the following:
- Constantly attempts to avoid real or imagined abandonment
- Unstable and intense relationships which tend to alternate between idealisation and devaluation
- Unstable self-image or sense of self
- Impulsivity (spending, sex, substance abuse, reckless driving, binge-eating)
- Recurrent threats or episodes of deliberate self-harm
- Instability of mood: rapidly changing in response to external events
- Chronic feelings of emptiness
- Intense anger and difficulty controlling anger
- Brief psychotic episodes (losing touch with reality) when under stress

Source: Adapted from DSM IV criteria (APA, 1994)

Clients with personality disorders can generate strong and often negative emotions not just among those who are close to them and their therapists but also in other caring professionals who have been drawn into dealing with a crisis, and even members of the criminal justice system. Those involved in care may be implored to 'do something' when it is in fact not possible to save from themselves clients who are unable to change. It is crucially important for a therapist to fully utilise supervision in exploring the range of feelings – from a desire to rescue, to rage and even fear – which may be engendered within the counter-transference. Personality disorder used to be considered untreatable, at least by most mainstream psychiatrists. This is not always easy for the general public to understand as they see a person, who is suffering and/or causing suffering to others, is clearly 'crazy' and 'should be helped'. However, this person may either not be able to accept such help or have the capacity to change. Psychotherapy is the treatment of choice, but change is often very difficult to achieve, if possible at all, and may take many years.

Which Psychiatric Conditions Might be Exacerbated by Counselling?

There has been considerable research in psychotherapy into factors associated with a poor outcome (Lambert and Ogles, 2003). There are strong indications that more severely disturbed people (particularly those who are 'psychotic') and those who could be described as 'borderline' (see above) do less well in psychotherapy. Some particularly aggressive styles or models of therapy which are confrontational may also break down needed defences in someone who otherwise appears to be coping with everyday life, at least superficially.

Anne is a counsellor in training who started personal therapy as part of her training requirements. All went well until Anne was encouraged to express very distressed feelings, following which she seemed to plunge into a very confused state of mind. The counsellor says this must be worked through but Anne is afraid; she seems to be getting worse and at times cannot cope with everyday routines.

Comment: If Anne feels afraid, confused, and is having difficulty maintaining a sense of the integrity of her everyday life this is an important warning sign that she is not coping with the therapy. The therapist should heed these warning signs and discuss the problem with her own supervisor. Perhaps the exploratory process needs to be taken at a gentler pace, or possibly the approach is too confrontational for Anne to cope with at this point. Anne should discuss her worries both with her counsellor and her own trainer. The possibility exists that Anne should not proceed with her own counselling training if the counselling process is threatening her own sense of integrity of 'self' in this way. She may benefit from assessment from a suitably well-experienced and qualified psychodynamic psychotherapist.

If a counsellor becomes involved in the care of someone with severe or 'borderline' personality difficulties it is crucially important that he or she is absolutely clear what the purpose, boundaries and limitations of the proposed sessions actually are. It is extremely easy to unwittingly get into a regressive relationship with such a client. Some therapists controversially encourage regression as part of the treatment they offer (Berke, 1979). In supervised insight-orientated therapy this may be entirely appropriate but if a counsellor is aiming to offer a brief intervention to enable the client to deal more effectively with current life problems this will be counterproductive. In some people who have a tenuous grip on reality, such as in 'borderline' personality disorder, the regression can become pathological and perhaps result in further disintegration or acting out of destructive feelings both inside and outside the counselling sessions. Clearly these issues and potentials should be addressed both in assessment and in supervision and, although many such clients are assessed as unsuitable for psychotherapy by mental health services, a counsellor can have a role to play in management as long as sessions are suitably tailored to the client's needs.

We would not deny the importance of support and understanding for a person who presents with symptoms of schizophrenia, nor deny that the presenting delusions and hallucinatory voices may be, like dreams, a reflection of thoughts and fears. However, the arousal caused by potentially uncovering material which the disturbed person may not be able to work with and use has led to a generally accepted belief that counselling is contraindicated other than at a supportive level. Counsellors sometimes find that, rather than working with the person suffering from schizophrenia, they can help a parent or spouse to come to terms with what can be a devastating family problem and in doing so hopefully helping to dispel the myth that the illness is in some way the 'fault' of the family. Although there is certainly no doubt that tension within the family can increase the likelihood of an acute relapse, by mechanisms not dissimilar to that by which counselling may cause this, the concept of a 'schizophrenogenic family' described by Laing and others in the 1960s (Laing and Esterson, 1970) has no basis in fact.

The other group of people who could be described as severely disturbed are those with severe depression and manic depressive illness. In both of these states it is important to recognise the early signs of deterioration. People with depression commonly seek, and benefit from, counselling, but there is no evidence for the efficacy of any form of psychological treatment in very severe depression. In both severe depression and mania the impact on thinking processes of the condition makes it increasingly difficult to work through things coherently in the way that is required in counselling. This is because in depression thinking is too slowed down and in mania too speeded up, the effect of both being to reduce the ability to focus and concentrate. There is even the risk that the severely depressed person will be disheartened by his or her failure to make progress and view this as more evidence of his or her deteriorating mental ability and lack of worth. In any event counselling might, unless these signs are detected and the style altered to a more supportive one, be at the least perceived as a negative experience and at worst be potentially harmful. For interesting personal accounts see Styron, 1992 and Sutherland, 1987.

Those with manic depressive illness can benefit from counselling but there is no evidence that this will decrease the likelihood of a relapse in their illness, whereas drug treatments have been demonstrated by research to prevent relapse. In both cases it is important to discuss with the client what he or she may be expected to gain from counselling and for the client to talk over as a separate issue, with the GP or psychiatrist as appropriate, the need to stay on medication. It is important that counselling does not cause deterioration in either of these conditions by delaying reassessment by the GP during the completion of the agreed number of sessions. The counsellor can be alert to and aware of potential signs of deterioration and in particular, with worsening depression, must be aware of, and assess, suicidal risk.

A Short Introduction to Psychotropic Medication

The most up-to-date information on psychotropic drugs (drugs which act on the brain) can be found in the British National Formulary (online at bnf.org). Here you can find essential information on:

- effective dose range
- side effects
- drug interactions.

Specific drug groups and the generic (pharmacological) and trade (proprietary) names of drugs can be found in Tables 6.15 to 6.18. When a drug goes off patent (usually after ten years on the market) companies other than the original manufacturer can produce it under the generic name at low cost. Withdrawal is much more difficult from drugs with a shorter 'half-life' and this includes Lorazepam and (in the antidepressants) notably Paroxetine (Seroxat). The half-life of a drug is the time taken for half of it to disappear from your system. There are three major groups of drugs that are used in mental health: the antidepressants (Table 6.15), the antipsychotic drugs also known as 'major' tranquillisers (Table 6.16) and the 'minor' tranquillisers (Table 6.17). The first major discoveries in these groups were all made in the 1950s and the next really important period came in the 1990s.

Antidepressants: Antidepressants may be helpful in combination with psychotherapy or counselling, particularly if the person is severely depressed, when they may be unable to formulate thoughts clearly and concentrate sufficiently to utilise talking treatments without additional medication. All of the antidepressants work by raising the level in the brain of a substance called serotonin which is a neurotransmitter, a molecule that carries messages in the brain. In severe depression, there is evidence that the level of serotonin in the brain drops. Raising the level takes time, so antidepressants do not work immediately but usually by two to three weeks. Some antidepressants (the tricyclics and the newer combined action drugs, venlafaxine and mirtazepine) also have an impact on another neurotransmitter called noradrenaline. In people who have bipolar disorder, antidepressants can trigger the onset of mania if used to treat depression without additional treatment with a 'mood stabiliser' such as Lithium, Sodium Valproate or Lamotrigine (see Table 6.18).

The first antidepressants commonly used were the tricyclics (see Table 6.15) but in the UK their use is being superseded by newer SSRIs (Selective Serotonin Reuptake Inhibitors) such as fluoxetine (Prozac) and Sertraline (Lustral). The tricyclics (TCAs) are effective but cause numerous side effects and can be lethal in overdose because they cause heart arrythmias and a lethal dose may be smaller than ten tablets. Thus they have generally been prescribed in small quantities, which can be a problem to people who have to pay for prescriptions. TCAs continue to be extensively used across the developing world because they work and they are extremely cheap. Another older group of antidepressants, the Monoamine Oxidase Inhibitors (MAOIs) are rarely used now outside specialist centres because of the multiple interactions that have with other drugs and with food (famously cheese).

The SSRIs arrived in the 1990s and prescriptions have increased dramatically, particularly to younger people who have not previously had antidepressants. They also have side effects but are generally easier to tolerate at effective doses than the older drugs. They may, however, cause significant irritability and agitation (which can, rarely, lead to suicide) and some have significant withdrawal reactions. This is not the same as addictiveness as antidepressants are not addictive in the sense that people do not psychologically crave them and so there is no dealing in them on the black market. However, when they are stopped, there may be a multitude of unpleasant symptoms including anxiety, aches and pains, headaches and flashing lights. **Withdrawal should therefore always be a gradual process**. The final addition to the antidepressants have been the newer 'combined action' drugs that work on both serotonin and noradrenaline, just like the TCAs did, but they are easier to take than the older drugs. These tend to be used when others (SSRIs) have failed. Venlafaxine (Efexor) also has a significant withdrawal syndrome.

Table 6.15   Antidepressants (commonly used types)

Used in: Depression, panic disorder, anxiety, Obsessive-compulsive disorder (SSRIs and clomipramine) Bulimia Nervosa (Fuoxetine)

Group name	Generic name	Proprietary name	Common side effects
SSRI	Citalopram	Cipramil	Nausea and vomiting agitation anxiety,
	Fluoxetine	Prozac	weight loss, dizziness, tremor, insomnia,
	Paroxetine	Seroxat	headaches, sweating, safe in overdose.
	Sertraline	Lustral	No weight gain
Tricyclic	Amitriptyline	*	Dry mouth, blurred vision, constipation,
	Clomipramine	Anafranil	urinary retention, Fits, heart arrythmias,
	Dothiepin	Prothiaden	weight gain. Generally dangerous in
	Imipramine	Tofranil	overdose except Lofepramine. Most
	Lofepramine	Gamanil	dangerous – dothiepin
Others	Mirtazepine	Zispin	Weight gain
	Venlafaxine	Efexor	Withdrawal syndrome and cardiac effects
			(NB: guidance has changed)
	Duloxetine		

*The tricyclics have been available for many years so it is unusual for anything other than generic versions to be prescribed. Fluoxetine is now also off patent so available generically

Antipsychotic drugs: These drugs (see Table 6.16) are mostly used in psychotic illness, schizophrenia or mania, but are also prescribed in smaller doses to control agitation in depression. Chlorpromazine (Largactil) is the best known of these, but is much less used now. Thioridazine (Melleril) used to be widely used for agitation in depression but was found to be responsible for sudden death through its impact on the heart and is now less used. Many people with a diagnosis of schizophrenia receive injectable drugs which have a prolonged action. In the late 1980s a drug that had been around for a long time, Clozapine (Clozaril), was discovered to have a significant impact on people with severe, previously drug-resistant illness. However, it also can cause serious blood problems and people receiving it require close monitoring. Newer 'atypical' antipsychotic drugs have appeared, which do not have the side effects of the older drugs, and current prescribing guidance from NICE (NICE, 2002) is that they should be available first-line. These drugs also have their own inherent problems such as increasing weight which has led to concern about the occurrence of diabetes in people on antipsychotic medication. Olanzepine can be effective in people with depression who have not otherwise responded to treatment. All the antipsychotic drugs may be used to treat agitation in severe depression but thioridazine is now only licensed for use in schizophrenia.

Drugs used in anxiety: The most well-known members of this group are the benzodiazepines ('benzos') diazepam (Valium) and Lorazepam (Ativan), which are prescribed much less than in the past for anxiety ('anxiolytics') because of their propensity to addiction, but are still going strong, particularly on the black market. New learning of the variety that is achieved in behavioural treatment for anxiety (particularly overcoming panic attacks) is difficult to achieve if the person is also taking anxiolytics, and it can be very unsatisfactory to try to work therapeutically with someone who is using benzodiaepines, as they are prevented from experiencing distress which may lead to change by the deadening effects of the medication.

Table 6.16   **Antipsychotic drugs (commonly used types)**

Group name	Generic name	Proprietary name	Common side effects
'atypical' antipsychotic drugs	Olanzapine Amisulpride Risperidone Quetiapine	Zyprexa Solian Risperdal	Movement disorders less common. Can cause weight gain
	Clozapine	Clozaril	Blood abnormalities – requires monitoring*
Older antipsychotics	Haloperidol Chlorpromazine Sulpiride Thioridazine Trifluoperazine	Haldol, Serenace Largactil Dolmatil Melleril Stelazine	Movement disorders: Parkinsonism (tremor/rigidity) Restless legs, spasms, movements of face and mouth. Drowsiness, rashes, sun
Injectable (long-acting)	Flupenthixol decanoate	Depixol	sensitivity, jaundice, fits, Menstrual problems, anaemias. Weight gain
	Fluphenazine decanoate	Modecate	
	Haloperidol decanoate	Haldol	

*People taking Clozapine require regular blood counts to monitor for serious blood side effects

This is considerably less true of the antidepressants as discussed above. However, there *may* be a place for very short-term treatment with benzodiazepines in acute crises or to enable a person to initially engage with potentially traumatic therapy and they are still used in short-term 'reducing regimes' (gradually decreasing dosage over several days) during withdrawal from alcohol.

Tom was asked to see a client, Gina, who had been experiencing anxiety and depression for several months following a severe bereavement reaction. Gina revealed to the counsellor that she had been obtaining diazepam from a dealer in her local pub. She was originally prescribed this after the death of her husband, but when her GP stopped prescribing she managed to obtain them elsewhere as she felt that she could not manage without. During the first couple of sessions Gina seemed rather flat and sedated. She expresses little emotion when talking about her husband and said that she did not want to feel any more pain. At times her thinking seems slowed up. Should Tom continue?

Comment: It will be difficult to help Gina to deal with her grief while she continues to use the diazepam. Tom needs to come to an agreement with Gina about the medication. He might ask that Gina sees the GP and starts a withdrawal regime. He might also consider entering into a contract which Gina agrees to withdrawal, in return for continuing work with Tom, but that if illicit use of diazepam continues sessions will cease. Tom will need to assess Gina's mood once she has been withdrawn from the diazepam, as it is a mood depressant in its own right, assess the degree of risk of suicide or self-harm on a regular basis and ensure that he has regular contact with Gina's GP for referral if needed.

Table 6.17   Drugs used in anxiety and as sleeping tablets (commonly used types)

Group name	Generic name	Proprietary name	Side effects
Benzodiazepines	Diazepam Chlordiazepoxide Lorazepam Alprazolam	Valium Librium Ativan Xanax	All very addictive. Can cause drowsiness and confusion
Beta blockers	Propranolol Oxprenolol	Inderal Trasicor	Light-headedness, sleep problems, nausea – not to be used in diabetes and certain types of chest disease
Buspirone 'Z' drugs	Buspirone Zaleplon Zopiclone	Buspar Sonata Zimovane	Also addictive – should not be used long-term

Beta blockers can be helpful for people with primarily physical symptoms of anxiety. They help performance, so are often used by people taking driving tests, or by professional musicians; they are banned in competitive snooker because they cause unfair advantage in steadying the hand holding the cue. They do not affect psychological symptoms such as worry, tension and fear, but do reduce physical symptoms of anxiety such as palpitations, sweating and tremor and they are not addictive.

Low doses of *tricyclic antidepressants* are also used for anxiety as they have the major advantage of being non-addictive, as have low doses of antipsychotic drugs, which may be used in anxiety. However, the latter carry the risk of long-term side effects, such as abnormal movements of the face and mouth (tardive dyskinesia) which can be seen in people who have been on the older antipsychotic drugs for some years and can be caused even by low doses.

Sleeping tablets: Benzodiazepines are still also used as 'hypnotics' (sleeping tablets), but the newest group of hypnotics are the 'Z' drugs which are not licensed for long-term use and do cause dependence in a number of people.

Drugs used to stabilize mood: People who have a diagnosis of bipolar disorder, as well as those who have depression which does not respond to antidepressants alone, or which recurs, may be prescribed a mood stabiliser (see Table 6.18). Lithium is the best known of these, and has been found to promote recovery in depression when given along with an antidepressant ('augmentation'). The major problems with Lithium are that it is potentially lethal in overdose and blood levels have to be checked regularly every three months to ensure that the level falls within the safe and the therapeutic range. High levels of Lithium can cause severe tremor and confusion, but a mild tremor and thirst are common side effects even at therapeutic doses. Lithium can also block the thyroid gland and cause hypothyroidism. The other mood stabilisers (apart from Lithium) are primarily used in epilepsy.

Helping a client to withdraw from tranquillisers: Many people in the community are dependent on minor tranquillisers. Counselling interventions have been demonstrated to decrease prescriptions for these drugs and they play an important part in the management of anxiety in primary care. The counsellor might be involved in helping the person who is dependent arrive at an informed decision about whether or not to attempt withdrawal and then supporting them through that

Table 6.18 Drugs used to stabilise mood

Group name	Generic name	Proprietary name	Common side effects
Lithium**	Lithium	Camcolit, Priadel	At normal levels: tremor, some thirst. Excess levels: thirst, vomiting, diarrhoea, tremor, confusion, death
Anticonvulsants	Sodium valproate Carbamazepine	Epilim, Depakote* Tegretol	

* Depakote is the version developed specifically for use in mental illness
** Blood levels should be checked regularly (at least every three months when stabilised) and renal and thyroid function every six months

process while they learn to face up to anxiety again and deal with it in other, healthier ways. Withdrawal means facing up to oneself again and learning how to cope with life's difficulties. Withdrawal regimes should be drawn up in conjunction with a GP or Community Mental Health Nurse. The person may decide initially to switch from a short-acting drug to a longer-acting one such as valium, before withdrawing, which is often easier for some than for others. See Hammersley (1995) for an excellent introduction to the counselling aspects of this.

Mental Health Law

Mental health law serves to formalise the removal of certain civil liberties from some people with serious mental health problems. There has always been differing but similar legislation across the countries of the UK, but with devolution some greater differences have emerged. A new Mental Health Act has been expected for some time in England and Wales and has been the subject of considerable debate. New mental health legislation was passed in Scotland in 2003 and a reasonably straightforward guide to this can be found at www.nes.scot.nhs.uk/mha. The Northern Ireland mental health legislation has some similarities with the English law of 1983 and dates from 1986. A succinct description can be found in Browne (2000).

England and Wales: The Mental Health Act (1983)
The sections of the Mental Health Act which are most likely to be met in practice are:

- Emergency and short-term orders for assessment for up to 28 days (Sections 2 and 4). These apply to any mental disorder which does not need to be specified.
- Longer-term orders for treatment (Section 3). These apply only to four specific types of disorder.

Mental illness is not defined but the Act states that a person should not be treated as suffering from mental disorder 'by reason only of promiscuity, or other immoral conduct, sexual deviancy or dependence on alcohol or drugs'. This means that a person cannot be detained in hospital simply on grounds of addiction but only if there is associated mental illness. For example, if the person is a drinker but also depressed and suicidal or in 'delerium tremens' (or DTs) because of withdrawal from alcohol and clearly hallucinating.

Severe mental impairment, which means learning disability associated with abnormal aggressive or seriously irresponsible conduct.

Mental impairment, which is similar to above but of lesser degree.

Psychopathic disorder, with associated aggressive conduct. The place of 'psychopathic disorder' in the Mental Health Act remains controversial and its use as a basis for 'sectioning' (a slang term in common usage which stands for detaining a person under the Act) depends on the notion of 'treatability' of the disorder. Mental health professionals are divided about whether it is possible to treat such severe personality disorders, as witnessed by the debate over recent high-profile cases. Use of the Act in detaining people with psychopathic disorder is largely restricted to the courts when imposing hospital treatment orders, which is covered in other sections of the Act and used to enforce treatment on mentally disordered offenders.

An *approved social worker* (ASW) is one approved by the local authority as having special experience of mental illness. Approved social workers undergo special training. An *approved doctor* is one who has been approved under Section 12 of the Act as having special experience of mental disorder and is usually a psychiatrist but can also be a GP who has had some experience in this field. Both now need to have attended brief training courses on the implementation of the law.

Section 2: Admission for assessment: This lasts up to 28 days. Application can be made by an ASW or the nearest relative and requires two doctors, one of whom must be approved and the other of whom should preferably know the patient, usually the GP. It is used to detain someone who is either a risk to themselves or to other people and needs admission to hospital. The patient has the right to appeal. In practice it is almost always now a social worker rather than a relative who actually makes the application in consultation with the family.

Section 3: Admission for treatment: This lasts up to six months in the first instance. Application can be made by an ASW or the nearest relative as before and requires the opinion of two doctors as for Section 2. In addition, the nature of disorder to be treated must be specified. It is used to detain someone who is either a risk to themselves or to other people and needs admission to hospital for treatment to be carried out. The patient has the right to appeal.

Section 4: Admission for assessment in case of emergency: This gives the police power to convey a person who appears to be in need of assessment to hospital. The use of this power is controversial and varies widely across the country. Common reasons for instituting it include assault, suicidal gestures, removing clothing in public places and 'bizarre' behaviour. A person cannot be 'sectioned' in order to treat physical illness although this has been the subject of recent controversial cases where unborn children are involved. Treatment can only be enforced for the mental disorder. Thus, if a person who is hearing voices refuses to have surgery, treatment can be provided for the 'voices' under the Act, for example by use of medication, but the surgery itself cannot be enforced.

The 1995 Mental Health (Patients in the Community) Act: This Act was introduced because of the recognition that the 1983 Act is based on admission to hospital and does not allow for people who refuse to continue treatment once they are discharged from hospital. It is undoubtedly hurried through because of public (and media) concern about the risk posed by the mentally ill living in the community and the much-publicised 'failure of community care'. This Act introduced the Supervised Discharge Order under which there is a community treatment agreement made with the patient before discharge. If the patient then defaults from treatment he or she can be conveyed under the Act to a treatment facility, but the Act does not provide any additional powers to enforce treatment or admission which must then be judged under the grounds set out in the 1983 Act.

Legal aspects of self-harm and medical care: A doctor may only administer treatment when a patient gives consent. A competent adult can reject medical or surgical treatment, or investigations, even if this is life-threatening. So a competent adult who has taken an overdose and who refuses treatment, in the knowledge of the potentially fatal risks, cannot be legally treated even if he or she becomes unconscious. The issue of whether a person has the *capacity* to make such a decision thus becomes crucial.

7

Safety and Safeguards

Introduction

This chapter offers broad and general guidance about good practice based on a consideration of current information. There is not scope here to offer comprehensive or definitive advice and all of us need to obtain professional or legal advice applicable to our own particular circumstances as the need arises. Fundamental to concerns about safety and safeguards in relation to medical and psychiatric issues is a general understanding of the current state of ethical and legal concerns in the counselling field. The foundation of these is to be found in the fields of medical law and ethics as outlined by texts such as those of Kennedy and Grubb (1994); Mason and McCall Smith (1994) and McClean (1995). More specifically with regard to counselling, Bond's (2000) book on ethics and Cohen (1992) and Jenkins' (1992; 1997) contributions on the law and counselling are particularly to be recommended.

The BACP Ethical Framework (BACP, 2002) is helpfully comprehensive and says that counsellors should be aware of and understand any legal requirements that relate to their work. BACP also publishes a comprehensive range of information leaflets which we shall draw on throughout this chapter. Concerns related to ethical and legal issues within counselling continue to grow as does those about complaints and litigation, often tempting us to practice in over-defensive ways. Such concerns also fuel the current pace of change of understanding in these areas. As practitioners we need to be aware of the current issues and developments in the areas of law, ethics and good practice and ensure that the implications of these are given full weight in the way we work. Although it is not possible to go into detail here, it is important to understand that some situations, such as consent, may apply differently to children (those under sixteen) and those under eighteen.

The whole area of compliance with ethical and legal requirements, especially the ones where there is uncertainty, has the potential to create a lot of anxiety in us. In the face of this, one temptation is to go into denial and to carry on practising in the same way. Another is to feel overwhelmed because the increase in workload involved feels unmanageable and the whole viability for practising becomes threatened. However, there are ways both of minimising the extra work involved to a manageable level and reducing the potentially disruptive effects on the work with clients. Also we must not lose sight of the fact that these laws are designed to bring protection to clients and can also offer it to us as well in many situations.

In recent years there has been a growth in situations in the medical and mental health arena in which people combine counselling skills with their other professional skills, such as graduate mental health workers and advocacy. Alongside the complementarity between skill in these areas, however, there exists the possibility that some of the assumptions that underlie the two activities may be in opposition, or that some activities may make others difficult or impossible. For example, assumptions within some counselling perspectives, such as promoting autonomy and using transference, can be undermined by advocate activity or other direct action which may introduce an element of dependence or passivity for the client or patient. The application of ethical principles and good practice within counselling to these areas is still relatively uncharted territory.

BACP Ethical Framework (BACP, 2002)

Most accredited counsellors in the UK work within this and so it is worth considering the parts of it that impact on work with medical and psychiatric issues in addition to the references made elsewhere. To a greater or less extent all the main six ethical principles impact on this area:

- fidelity: honouring the trust placed in the practitioner
- autonomy: respect for the client's right to be self-governing
- beneficence: a commitment to promote the client's well-being
- non-malevolence: a commitment to avoiding harm to the client
- justice: the fair and impartial treatment of all clients and the provision of adequate services
- self-respect: fostering the practitioner's self-knowledge and care for self.

There are a number of detailed principles in the framework that are worth highlighting with reference to medical and psychiatric matters. Providing a good quality of care requires that practitioners are appropriately supported and accountable. It is important to take account of what other services are available that the client might need and to take into account that their absence may constitute a significant limitation. Good practice also involves keeping up to date with the latest knowledge and changes in circumstances. Counsellors also need to undergo continuing professional development and to engage in appropriate educational activities.

Duty of Care

The exact meaning of duty of care in relation to counselling is not very clear compared with that applying to the medical profession. Part of the reason for that is the lack of litigation and consequent paucity of case law and an increase in litigation would be a high price to pay for clarity. The counsellor's duty of care can best be summarised by saying she is under an obligation to carry out her work with reasonable care and skill. This clearly includes working with medical and psychiatric matters and means that we will be judged according to the current standards of the profession in this area. These standards include guides to ethics and practice, the main texts on the subject, and the views of leading practitioners (see Cohen, 1992). In general we must ensure that we are competent, not negligent, not reckless and offer a service of an appropriate standard. It is important to note that part of competence is to ensure that our own health is compatible with meeting the required professional standards with clients. The BACP Ethical Framework (BACP, 2002) says that practitioners should monitor and maintain their fitness to practise at a level that enables them to provide an effective service, including the effects of health and personal circumstances. In some circumstances a withdrawal from working may be needed until fitness returns.

Currently the general standard for judging counsellors in their management of medical and psychiatric issues is in terms of what is *widely* practised, but it is important to be aware that there is a trend towards considering *best-known* practice as the yardstick in discussions of this area. We have emphasised the importance of carrying out a fairly formal and structured assessment of clients when they are seen for the first time. However, we recognise that many counsellors do not practise in this way and that they experience a conflict between the values that underlie their theoretical orientation and such practice. The process of assessment in such approaches takes place over a longer period as material emerges during sessions. It is important that counsellors recognise that additional risks attach to ways of working that cannot clearly identify medical and psychiatric risks at the beginning of counselling.

Therefore counsellors need in their contracting and arrangements with clients to clarify their role in relation to any existing medical and psychiatric conditions and to make clear the rights and responsibilities of both the client and the counsellor when these arise during the course of ongoing work (see Kennedy, 1988: 125; BACP, 2002). In order to do this effectively, it is necessary to clearly establish what treatment the client might already be having. Clients vary in the degree to which they volunteer information, either because they have reasons to be concerned about revealing it, or because they do not think it relevant. As a result counsellors need to be proactive in asking rather than assuming that the information they need will emerge.

> Janet had anxieties about confidentiality which reflected an underlying problem of lack of trust. The counsellor had worked over a number of sessions to build up trust when Janet disclosed concerns over visual symptoms and headaches which concerned the counsellor. She suggested to Janet that she talk to her GP, but she said that she felt better now that she had talked about things and did not want to go to the doctor. The counsellor asked her if she could discuss these concerns herself with the doctor and Janet responded in a very agitated way and refused permission. The counsellor asked advice from colleagues and concluded that she had a duty of care towards the patient which meant that she had at least to discuss the symptoms with one of the doctors but without at this stage disclosing the name of the patient.

In order for negligence to be proved, it has to be proved that the counsellor owed a duty of care, that the counsellor's conduct did not conform to the appropriate standard of care and that harm resulted from this. Where disagreement exists as to how a particular situation involving medical or psychiatric conditions is best handled, we are less likely to be open to legal action if we act in ways that would find support amongst a reasonable proportion of responsible practitioners. It is important to be aware, though, that any departing from generally accepted practice will always carry risks. Practice using unconventional or untried approaches to a problem is likely to be more difficult to defend when something goes wrong than if such consequences follow on from a more accepted approach.

Suicidal and Violent Risk

The same criteria of appropriate standards of care apply in the tragic situation when a client commits suicide, and the three factors that are likely to be crucial in determining whether there has been negligence are whether (Daly, 1993):

- the client's suicide was foreseeable
- if the suicide risk was known or should have been inferred by the counsellor, the counsellor took the appropriate precautionary measures
- the counsellor offered help in a reliable and dependable way.

Counsellors need to be aware of the current body of knowledge about suicide and self-harm and in particular methods of assessing the degree of risk, such as the widely used CORE which can usefully flag-up risk issues (CORE, 1998; see also Eldrid, 1988). Bond (2000) summarises the factors that therapists need to consider and distinguishes three groups; those who are competent to make their own decisions, those whose capacity is in doubt because of their mental state, and those at highest risk who lack the capacity to understand the consequences of their actions. Reeves and Seber (BACP Information sheet P7) say that the most helpful course of action for the counsellor to take will depend on many factors, including the context in which the therapy is taking place, the relationship with the client, the boundaries of confidentiality agreed, and the confidence of the therapist to explore the meaning of suicide.

Part of the appropriate standard of care for all clients involves respecting their autonomy and right to confidentiality and it is easy for these to be compromised in a stressful and anxiety provoking situation. Striking the balance between the ethical responsibilities of respecting autonomy and confidentiality on the one hand, and protecting clients from self-destruction on the other, is usefully discussed by Bond (1993). His conclusion is that generally 'the best practice with regard to suicidal clients works in ways which respect the client's autonomy and right to choose until there are substantial grounds for doubting a client's capacity to take responsibility for himself; and there is a serious risk of suicide and there is the possibility of an alternative way of intervening' (p. 122). Working within similar care settings, GPs often refer clients who have a history of taking action in response to a suicidal state (Reeves and Seber, BACP Information sheet P7): this example shows that consulting other specialists is normal practice and does not denote a failure.

Bond argues that careful assessment of the situation not only provides the best basis for making decisions about suicidal clients, but also provides evidence that duty of care has been honoured. He also discusses many areas of ethical concern with suicidal clients including those that may arise after a client's suicide (Bond, 2000). Whilst many counsellors have anxieties about this eventuality, with good management of clients who express suicidal feelings, the actuality is rare. Where it does happen it is important to be aware that the coroner's court may require a report, or attendance at an inquest, or both. We need to be aware of the effect of working with suicidal clients as, not surprisingly, studies suggest that this is one of the most difficult therapeutic issues that counsellors face (Rudd *et al.*, 1999).

Most counsellors will work with suicidal clients at some point in their career and this can produce various symptoms of stress as well as a feeling of lack of professional competence (Reeves and Mintz, 2001; Richards, 2000). Fox and Cooper (1998) identify several ways in which this operates. A perception of failure to recognise warning signs can lead to guilt and shame and there can be fears associated with the possibilities of blame and litigation. The BACP Ethical Framework states that 'the therapist's wellbeing is essential to sustaining good practice' (BACP, 2002) and it is important that counsellors take action to restore such well-being when working with this group of clients.

Mike, a retired man in his late fifties, had a long history of depression and alcohol problems before coming for counselling. He had recently retired from his work as an accountant in the NHS and his wife left him shortly after this which is what prompted him to seek help. In the first session with Anna he disclosed that he had often felt suicidal in the past and was feeling particularly so at present. His CORE scores confirmed that there was cause for concern and led her to ask him whether he had made specific plans and preparations. His responses to this were evasive. Anna decided to ask him for permission to talk to the GP who had referred him and he was happy to give permission. Talking to the GP resulted in a review of his antidepressant medication and an urgent referral to psychiatry which still meant a couple of months wait for an appointment. Over the next few weeks Mike became more positive and, when asked, said that his suicidal feelings had more or less gone away. One Monday Mike did not arrive for his appointment and Anna learnt later that day that he had committed suicide by hanging.

This led Anna into much soul-searching. Had she missed anything in the last session that might have indicated his intentions? She explored this and other questions with her supervisor. Their conclusion was that Anna had managed the risk well and that this eventuality could not have been foreseen at the point where it happened. They recognised that Mike's age, isolation and recent divorce put him in a group very vulnerable to suicide. Anna was asked to submit a statement to the Coroner about her work with Mike but was not called to give evidence at the inquest.

In relation to violent risk counsellors have a responsibility to protect themselves as well as others. Work with high risk clients needs to be carried out in a safe setting, which involves not only suitable premises and adequate staffing levels, but also comprehensive risk assessment and management protocols. All counsellors need to be able to assess violent risk and need to be familiar with the kinds of mental health problems and mental states that are most associated with this risk. This area is covered in more detail by Jackson (BACP Information Sheet G5). Jenkins *et al.* (2004) point out that the law in England and Wales takes a restricted view of the liability of counsellors and psychotherapists for harm to third parties.

Stalking never seems to be out of the press and there have been a number of high profile cases, such as Madonna and Jodie Foster. It has also established a place in popular culture through films such as *Fatal Attraction* and *Enduring Love*. There is a growing body of literature in this area including general introductions (e.g. Mullen *et al.*, 2000) and aids to assessment in this area (Davis and Chipman, 1997; Davis *et al.*, 1999; Meloy, 2001; Meloy *et al.*, 2001). What are less well publicised, however, are the cases involving counsellors, psychotherapists and psychologists (Meloy, 2000; Romans *et al.*, 1996; Sandberg *et al.*, 1998). Delusional stalkers are both threatened by and yearn for closeness and so often pick victims who are unattainable in some way. The activities of those in the helping professions make them particularly vulnerable to certain kinds of stalkers as their dealings with clients can be developed into a delusion of intimacy. The dangers are greater for the inexperienced counsellor who might allow an idealisation to develop too far and too easily accept the view that they are the answer to the client's needs. Lonely or vulnerable counsellors are even more at risk if they are unaware of their problems and communicate them to the client at an unconscious level (Morgan, 1999). When working with socially isolated loners who are unable to establish or sustain close relationships, there is a need to carefully monitor idealisations, erotic transferences and fantasies that the counsellor has hidden feelings for the client.

Confidentiality

The area of confidentiality is one of the most difficult ethical areas because it involves balancing a number of issues which have a strong ethical dimension. These include respecting client autonomy, informed consent, duty of care to the client and others, and safeguarding the reputation of the client. Jamieson and Bond (BACP Information Sheet G2) say that counsellors who seek to inform themselves in more detail about the current law on confidentiality will encounter a number of difficulties, particularly as the law of confidentiality is evolving rapidly and has been substantially widened. The second difficulty they identify is the absence of any single coherent approach to confidentiality, especially in Britain where the tendency of courts is to take a flexible approach to problems as they arise. This leaves the legal responsibility with the counsellor to use professional judgement according to the circumstances of the case. The BACP Ethical Framework (2002) places importance on the counsellor's judgement in balancing disclosing or maintaining confidentiality in relation to potential harm to the client. The fundamental dilemma for the counsellor as described by Reeves and Seber (BACP Information Sheet P7) is between the danger of being sued by the client for breach of confidence in relation to damage to reputation and the dual risks of failure to follow organisational procedures and failure in duty of care. These issues are more fully discussed by Bond (2000) and Jenkins (1997).

The following comments are based on the discussion of confidentiality and record-keeping by Cohen (1992: 19–24). It is important to recognise that consent to disclose is not generally an absolute. For example, it may be confined to specific information and it will generally only be to a specific third party, or limited number of parties. The purpose of the discussion requiring disclosure should be made clear to the client, as should that disclosures from the counsellor will be limited to those that are necessary to the matters in hand. A dilemma can arise where the counsellor knows that disclosure must take place, such as where the client's life, or that of someone else, is at risk. In such an instance should the counsellor try to persuade the client to give consent? This goes against most counsellors' ideas about respecting their clients' autonomy. However, such persuasion may be seen as valuing autonomy more than not making the attempt to obtain permission and just going ahead with disclosure.

It is generally accepted that in certain emergencies it may not be possible to obtain permission for disclosure. However, where it happens without consent, it is relevant to whom the disclosure is made. To put this in an extreme form, disclosure to a client's GP would be seen very differently from disclosure to the press! A defence for disclosure is where the public interest served by disclosure is greater than that served by maintaining confidentiality, but there are no clear guidelines for weighing this balance. In a particular instance there is no way of knowing in advance how a court might rule on a matter.

One aspect that is clear is that counsellors cannot legally offer absolute confidentiality; neither can the limits to confidentiality be totally clearly defined. It is also important to note that current practice indicates that damages for emotional distress following on from breach of confidence may be awarded if the client pays the counsellor directly, but not if the counsellor is a volunteer or paid by a third party such as the NHS. Counsellors also need to clarify for themselves the status of their records and notes in their work setting. In particular they need to be clear who owns these notes and who has, or potentially may have, access to them. Finally, some aspects of consent to disclose may be implied. For example, in a GP surgery there is an assumption that information given to a receptionist by a client can be passed on to the practice counsellor.

Carlo, a counsellor who happened to be in the office at the time, answered the telephone at the centre one Tuesday afternoon.

'Hello, Valley Counselling. Can I help you?'

'Yes, it's Ken Wilson here. I know that my wife sees one of your counsellors this morning and I will be in the area later on so could you tell me what time she finishes. Then I can give her a lift home'.

'I am sorry that we cannot give out information about people who see us'.

'I know – but I am her husband and it will save her having to come home on the bus'.

'I am sorry but it's still not possible to discuss it with you'.

'I have got the right place haven't I? – her name is Brenda Wilson and I think she sees someone called Pat'

'Because of confidentiality we cannot let anyone know who does or does not come here for counselling'.

'This is ridiculous!'

'I can understand why you might see it that way but our professional organisation requires that we operate very strict confidentiality in the interest of all our clients'.

(Rings off.)

This example shows the safeguarding of the confidentiality of the client's counselling. Whilst superficially it might seem extreme and not in the interests of the client, Carlo knows nothing about the client's circumstances and whether the person on the telephone is who he says he is or, if he is, whether the client wants a lift home from him.

Negligent Advice

The giving of unsound advice opens up the counsellor to action for negligence as also does the failure to give appropriate advice (Cohen, 1992: 15). This means that counsellors who suspect that there may be an organic or psychiatric cause behind something that a client is discussing, or observe symptoms that concern them, should discuss with the client the advisability of consulting his GP if this has not already happened. Because of lack of precedent, it is not entirely clear that failure to do so would be actionable, but the risk is best avoided. It is likely that those who work in medical settings are potentially more open to action than those who do not.

Competence

We must avoid stepping outside our limits of competence and this involves a degree of self-monitoring and the seeking of the views of others. 'Practitioners should give careful consideration to the limitations of their training and experience and work within these limits, taking advantage of available professional support' (BACP, 2002). Counsellors need to ensure that their views about their limits to competence in medical and psychiatric matters are not at odds with those of relevant others such as supervisors, managers, professional bodies and insurers. This does not just mean considering the generally accepted limits to competence for counsellors, but also those applying to someone of the counsellor's own training and experience in their own particular setting. Employed counsellors certainly need to discuss such issues with their line manager, and those working in independent practice need to be aware that this may be an arena in which they are more likely to be vulnerable and so arrange adequate support.

It is not only important to have supervision and consultancy arrangements set up, but also for the nature and frequency of these to be appropriate. The amount of supervision needs to be related to caseload, and the question of minimum frequency is important because this limits how long a situation can 'drift' without there being an opportunity to talk to a supervisor about it. Supervisees also need to monitor how often supervision actually happens as what on paper may seem to be an adequate frequency can become inadequate when holidays, illness and other interruptions are taken into consideration. Also supervisees need to ensure that medical and psychiatric concerns in their clients are regularly brought into supervision.

Even over the course of a week a person's physical or psychological state can seriously deteriorate and this is where consultancy arrangements can be valuable, either as an adjunct to discussing the client in supervision, or in preference as specialised advice is needed. A situation where advice relating to serious medical or psychiatric concerns for a client can be obtained the same day would be ideal. Some voluntary organisations recruit medical practitioners onto their management committees specifically for this purpose. Individual practitioners can often set up some arrangement through their network of professional relationships and this can be usefully established on a reciprocal basis where the other person needs access to advice about counselling matters. For example, one of the authors has informal arrangements with a GP and a psychiatrist whereby he can ask for advice about medical or psychiatric matters and they can ask his advice about patients. In such arrangements it is important that issues of boundary and confidentiality are clear.

> Sandra came to her supervision session with Penny very distressed about what had been happening at work. She reported that over the last few months she had been making a number of mistakes and that there had now been complaints both from the receptionist and from clients. On a number of occasions she had omitted to fill appointments or had booked two people in. Also she had called one client by the wrong name and muddled names in people's histories leading to the client becoming upset or angry at her not remembering correctly. Sandra was 63 and was hoping to work until she was 65. At a recent meeting with her clinical manager there had been a suggestion that she might retire early and this had really upset her. Sandra had not mentioned these things before in supervision because she was ashamed of the mistakes she was making.
>
> Penny helped her to look at the fact that she had taken on a lot of responsibilities for older relatives as well as having anxieties about her partner and her adult children that were not likely to change in the foreseeable future, and could possibly become worse. Sandra agreed with this and they explored how currently she was overloaded with caring for others. Penny suggested that she needed not only to think about what she wanted for herself and her career, but also whether she was able to maintain her competence at a satisfactory level for clients. Sandra agreed to discuss things further with her manager and at the next supervision session.

Counsellors must be careful not to give medical or psychiatric advice or treatment. At first glance this may seem to be straightforward, but in reality the boundary can easily become blurred. What should the counsellor do if a client requests paracetamol for a headache? If someone falls over on the way to a session, should the counsellor administer first aid? It is sensible for counsellors not to give or recommend to clients anything that might be considered a drug, however innocuous. Similarly counsellors should refrain from making recommendations or giving advice about ceasing or resuming prescribed medication. In medical emergencies counsellors should not attempt first aid beyond their competence, and all organisations and establishments should have someone responsible for first aid facilities, and preferably also someone with recognised training. Organisations are covered by health and safety legislation in this area as well as any policies operated by the organisations themselves.

Informed Consent

This has become more important in recent years because of clarification of what is involved in informed consent and the Human Rights Act 1998. In terms of complaints and litigation against the medical profession, lack of informed consent has become much more prominent than negligence in duty of care. This is because the onus is on the complainant to prove negligence but on the professional to show that informed consent was given. Informed consent must be obtained from all clients for counselling, not only at assessment or the beginning of therapy but at any point where there is a significant change in approach, in risk or any practical arrangements.

Informed consent involves the following:

- assessing that clients have the capacity to give informed consent
- consent must be given voluntarily, i.e. it must be free from coercion. It is important therefore not to seek to persuade clients to consent and to ensure that they are not attending because of pressure from, for example, family or a GP
- consent must be informed in the sense that clients must be given sufficient information on the potential benefits and disadvantages and risks that are material to their particular situations.

The first aspect, assessing that clients have the capacity to give informed consent has three components:

- assessing that clients can understand and retain the information given
- assessing that the client's grasp on reality is sufficient for them to believe what is being said
- assessing that clients can weigh up and balance the information given to come to an informed decision.

Where the issue of consent comes into conflict with others, such as the management of risk, a decision has to be made about which principle takes priority. This decision about priority should be based on principles consistent with the Human Rights Act 1998, codes of ethics and practice, and any other relevant policies and protocols. An example is the waiving one or more of the requirements for informed consent because the risks of discontinuing (e.g. suicidal, violence, child protection) override the need for consent to be informed. The use of the Human Rights Act in this kind of context is discussed below.

In practical terms the first thing the counsellor must do is assess whether the client can orientate to reality enough to give consent. The most likely situations where this may not be the case are where there is extreme distress or a psychotic state. This means that counsellors must be able to recognise and assess that a client is not sufficiently orientated to reality and also judge what constitutes a sufficient degree of distress that someone is unable to process what is needed to make an informed decision. It is helpful to us that English law assumes that adults are in a position to give consent unless the opposite is apparent. On any consent matter the counsellor must clearly explain what is being suggested and the potential benefits, disadvantages and risks to the client, both in general terms and those that apply to the particular person. The client needs then to be asked whether they feel they understand what has been said, and whether they think they can weigh up the issues and come to a decision. Counsellors must avoid persuading client to accept any proposed help or change in approach. It is important to fully document the informed consent including what is being offered and why and the potential benefits, disadvantages and risks both in general terms and the ones that apply to the particular client.

This process must be applied to any action taken about medical or psychiatric matters, such as:

- taking on someone for counselling in relation to a psychiatric or medical condition

- including treatment of a psychiatric or medical condition which has emerged into an existing counselling contract
- requesting or arranging for a medical or psychiatric assessment
- responding to a client's medical or psychiatric emergency.

Arian came to the first session with Anna in a state of extreme distress because her partner and father of her ten-month-old baby had left the previous evening. She had not thought there was anything wrong with their relationship apart from the pressure caused by a young baby who did not sleep well at night. However, the previous evening her partner announced that he had had enough of her moodiness and tiredness and lack of interest in sex and he was leaving. When Arian asked him whether there was anyone else he initially denied it but then said that he had been having an affair with someone at work for the previous six months.

Arian was devastated and became progressively more upset as the session went on. When asked by Anna whether she would like to attend for a weekly session she said she did not know what she wanted. Anna's judgement was that she was not in an emotional state where she could give informed consent to counselling and proposed another session where this could be sorted out. Arian was also clearly reluctant to give consent to that, but Anna felt that it was important to put another appointment in the diary despite this because of Arian's current vulnerability and the fact that she had the sole care of her baby.

Human Rights Act 1998

The Human Rights Act 1998 came into force in 2000 and relates to any situation where an individual's rights are involved. All those whose work impinges on people's rights need training in the way in which this Act affects their decision-making at work. The guidance in this section should not be seen as a substitute for such training. The articles in the Act fall into three categories: absolute, limited and qualified rights. An absolute right cannot be restricted in any way or under any circumstances. A limited right contains circumstances in which the right can be infringed without the article being breached. Qualified rights include the provision for a balance to be achieved between the rights of an individual and those of others. There are two main clauses that potentially impact on the decisions of counsellors dealing with medical and psychiatric issues. The first is a limited right, Article 5, which says that everyone has the right to liberty and security, but that one of the exceptions to this is detention of persons 'of unsound mind, alcoholics or drug addicts or vagrants'. The second is a qualified right, Article 8, which says that everyone has the right for respect for his private family life, but that there can be interference with the exercise of this right for the protection of health, or for the protection of the rights of others. Any interference with a qualified right must be proportionate, which means that the restriction on the right must not go further than is necessary.

Any decision can be taken through a logical step-by-step process. The first of these is whether the decision is going to affect someone's human rights. If the answer to this is affirmative, then the next steps are to establish whose rights and what rights. Once the rights are identified it is necessary to ask whether they are absolute or qualified rights. If they are not absolute is there a law that allows me to interfere with that right? If so, does the interference fit with one of the qualifications? Finally, if it does fit it is necessary to judge whether my proposed interference is proportionate. An example will help clarify this process.

Imagine that a client has presented with a report of symptoms that has led the counsellor to believe that he may have a serious physical condition. Part of the work of the counselling has been to do with a suspicion of authority, and in particular of doctors. Discussing the issues with the client has made it clear that he does not want to see the doctor and does not want the counsellor to talk to her either. The counsellor is now faced with the decision of whether to talk to the doctor herself. This action would clearly affect someone's human rights – the client's. The right that would be affected would be that of the right to a private life, but this is a qualified right. Also the interference proposed with that right would fit in with one of the qualifications – the protection of health. The final decision is whether the interference is proportionate, and this is not clear. If the symptoms turn out, in the opinion of the doctor not to be serious, then confidentiality and trust have been broken to no good effect. On the other hand, if the counsellor's suspicions about the seriousness of the situation are confirmed, there is no guarantee that this will result in the client seeking medical help. However, whatever the counsellor decides in the end in this case can be supported by a logical account in relation to the Human Rights Act. It is not always necessary for us to be right, especially in complex situations, but it is necessary for us to show that we have acted knowledgeably and with care in the processes we have gone through to reach our conclusions.

Ethical Dilemmas Arising in Medical Settings

In medical settings, the responsibilities of the counsellor will include not only those arising out of the counselling setting but also those arising from being part of the practice or unit (Higgs and Dammers, 1992). One important difference between the counsellor and the rest of the team is that a different understanding of confidentiality is likely to apply. Specifically there may be an assumption that all knowledge and notes are at least potentially available to the team.

Consequently there may be an expectation that the counsellor will automatically make available to others disclosures that might affect the clinical judgement of colleagues in dealing with the patient. The counsellor will approach disclosure much more from the point of view of what really has to be disclosed for the patient's or other's safety, than whether other members of the team might find it informative. An allied assumption may be that the counsellor needs to know all the available clinical details on a patient, even those that the patient is not aware of herself. We have already discussed the problem of unwelcome disclosures that can cloud the focus of the counselling from the counsellor's perspective.

It is important that the client's medical practitioner is clear as to the kind or the degree of help the counsellor is offering to the client. It is better for the counsellor to convey information directly as needed, rather than relying on the client to relay accurately what is being offered. Such communications should be clear and not rest on any assumptions about what the GP should be expected to know about the way counsellors in general or particular organise their work, or the perspective they take.

The counsellor also needs to ensure that promises made by her colleagues about the effects of, or the efficacy of counselling, in relation to medical or psychiatric conditions, are not exaggerated or misleading. Where this happens it is generally because of lack of knowledge or misunderstandings and, especially where counselling is a new part of the service, the counsellor must be prepared to invest a considerable amount of time and energy in educating her colleagues where they are not familiar with counselling. In all these areas it is important that such differences in perspective and boundaries are clarified before they arise in relation to clients. Hopefully, where counselling is an established part of the service, guidelines will have been carefully worked out and made available to new counsellors. Problems are more likely to arise where a counselling service is being established for the first time in a medical setting.

Counsellors finding themselves involved in developing such services need to be aware of the difficulties and be prepared both to understand the working culture of the existing service and argue the legitimacy of the specific conditions and boundaries that counselling requires if it is going to be ethical and effective. For clarity, and for future reference, it is desirable that protocols are put in writing so that the context within which the counsellor is working in the organisation is clear to everyone.

Those working in medical settings also need to be aware that their vulnerability to action following a complaint may in certain instances be greater than for others. Cohen says that: 'Counsellors who suspect an organic cause for their clients' emotional problems should therefore, as a matter of good practice, discuss with the clients the advisability of having a medical examination. Whether a failure to do so would be actionable remains to be seen, and would probably depend on the setting in which the counselling took place' (1992: 16). Where counsellors become aware of possible negligence or unprofessional behaviour on the part of colleagues in their team there will normally be a responsibility to take action about this. Appropriate advice about action can often be obtained from the counsellor's professional body or insurers.

Counselling in Medical Settings, a division of BACP, has produced a valuable set of guidelines for the employment of counsellors in general practice (Ball, 1993). These offer recommendations about how counsellors should work as part of a primary health care team, including the importance of team members understanding each other's roles and resources. They advise that the practice and the counsellor work together in developing a protocol for the service. In the area of confidentiality, discussed elsewhere in this chapter, the need for some sharing of information is recognised, but the emphasis is put on negotiating this with clients and not merely assuming it.

Complaints

The area of complaints is one that continues to grow in importance. The kind of trauma experienced by counsellors when a complaint is made is such that it can be tempting to either practice very defensively or try to avoid mentioning the issue with clients. Over-defensive practice rarely enables the counsellor to be available to clients in a way that is likely to offer them a good experience of the counselling relationship. Also, there is a responsibility to take seriously the clients' rights in this area and to provide them with the appropriate information they need to pursue dissatisfactions and to make complaints (Jenkins, 1992: 166). Some professional bodies expect all clients to be informed at the outset of where they can obtain the code of ethics, code of practice and complaints procedure that apply to the counsellor. Where complaints are made in medical settings there is a potential for some confusion as, for example in the case of practice counselling, the complaint may come to the counsellor's professional body, the GP practice or the primary care trust. Sometimes a similar complaint may be made to more than one body simultaneously.

The Position of Supervisors

The position of supervisors in relation to the ethical issues we have discussed is potentially a difficult one as they have responsibility for the welfare of the super-visees' clients as well as for their supervisees. Whilst the counsellor is clearly the one who is primarily responsible for her work with clients, situations can arise where this is not being fulfilled and the supervisor comes to believe that the situation cannot be resolved purely through supervision. Such situations will include serious mental illness and serious physical signs or symptoms. In such cases a supervisor may need to take action, but should take careful advice, for example from their supervisor or a consultant, before taking action. Discontinuing supervision in the face of a supervisee's bad practice is not considered to adequately discharge a supervisor's responsibilities, and may open up the way to disciplinary action on the matter being taken against the supervisor. Unfortunately the clarification of these areas in relation to supervision is even less developed than for counselling, and supervisors must accept that they operate in areas of responsibility that are not currently clearly defined.

Conclusion

Whilst sound ethical and legal principles can be applied to the medical and psychiatric dilemmas that emerge during counselling it has to be recognised that much of this has not been tested out in practice. This should not unduly perturb counsellors, however, provided they operate within the best practice of the profession, including good training and ongoing supervision and professional development. It is important to make detailed contemporaneous written records in cases where there is potential difficulty or where usual practice is not followed.

Situations are often difficult because they involve a conflict in ethical principles which makes the way forward unclear. Consultation with supervisors and colleagues is important in attempting to resolve such areas of conflict. Usually the way forward in relation to an ethical dilemma emerges out of discussions with, and advice from, more than one person. Even where ethical decisions involving the medical and psychiatric arena need to be made quickly, it is important to try to talk to at least one other person about the matter before acting, as this will often bring an important perspective to the situation. Sometimes problems that at first appear to need immediate action on reflection do not appear so urgent, and further time is then available before having to act. It is often helpful to include in your discussions someone who you think might not agree with you as a safeguard against action based on a collusive process. Where a situation is a serious one, advice from insurers and an independent legal source should be considered.

Considering ethical and legal issues raises anxieties that can potentially feel unmanageable. This is especially so where medical and psychiatric matters are involved. In the face of all this the greatest danger is the adopting of a 'head in the sand' attitude or hoping for the best that difficult situations will never arise. With adequate knowledge, clear thinking and good support it is possible to deal with these issues in a way that safeguards both the client and the counsellor. It is important to have ways of maintaining up-to-date knowledge in these areas and to have sources of information, advice and support identified before a difficulty arises. For example, in finding a supervisor consideration can be given to what areas of expertise they might have in these areas and their practical experience of dealing with difficult ethical situations and the management of complaints.

8 Conclusion

Medical and psychiatric issues have the potential to create a lot of anxiety in counsellors. This is especially so when aspects of this are related to compliance with codes of ethics and practice and legal requirements, particularly in areas where there is uncertainty about what exactly 'compliance' might mean. The situation becomes even more complex for those who work in more than one setting or belong to more than one professional body, especially when aspects of practice are different. They can be experienced as unwelcome issues coming as additions to the already considerable requirements of the policies and procedure of the setting in which they work.

The danger in coming to the end of a book such as this is that the issues to be addressed can seem overwhelming. In the face of this one response can be to experience the potential increase of workload involved as unmanageable and the whole possibility of safe practice as being threatened. This is particularly so for whom the changes are seen as posing a threat to their philosophy of counselling and the theoretical basis underlying their work. Another and somewhat opposite response is to employ a kind denial and carry on practising in the same way, hoping for the best. It is our view that the first of these viewpoints is overly pessimistic and that the second is reckless and potentially negligent once deficiencies in practice have been identified. Indeed, for those who work in medical settings where standards of care have been subject to increasing scrutiny through the development of clinical governance this is simply not an option. However, whilst there is much to consider, this is limited by the fact that everything does not apply to every client or every counselling setting. In fact there will be many clients for whom medical and psychiatric issues are marginal or non-existent. The activity of the counsellor in these areas in relation to this group of clients will be confined to discovering this at assessment and ongoing monitoring of whether such issues need to be addressed.

There will be a smaller group of clients for whom these areas are very relevant, but where they can be dealt with by the counsellor in a relatively straightforward way. These include clients who need referral for assessment in a medical or psychiatric setting and those for whom liaison with a GP or other involved party is needed from time to time. Inevitably there will be a minority whose medical or psychiatric problems cause concern for the counsellor, or who are difficult to manage because of these issues. From time to time these clients can consume a great deal of time and energy in activities such as thinking through the issues, consulting books and articles, using the internet for information, consulting other professionals, writing letters and making phone calls, obtaining advice from managers and talking things through in supervision. Clients of this kind may appear more in certain settings than others and it is important that as far as possible counsellors ensure their caseload is not overloaded with difficulties of this nature.

However, there are ways both of reducing the extra work involved and minimising the potentially disruptive effects on counselling. One of these is to avoid haphazard thinking and avoid feeling overwhelmed by developing clear paths of thinking about the medical and psychiatric aspects of the work. In this the use of protocols can be valuable in areas such as the management of risk and making decisions about consulting others for advice. Whilst these have their primary value in organisational settings, there is value for those who work independently or in isolation to also adopt these. Protocols not only guide thought and action but reduce the task of recording by references to clauses in them so that actions do not have to be described each time in full.

The role of support and consultation is crucial and we do not apologise for mentioning it again here. The importance of regular clinical supervision cannot be over-emphasised and despite its prominence we are aware that it is not uncommon for situations to arise where particular clients are never discussed. It is also not unusual for long gaps in supervision to occur because, for example, the holiday of the supervisor is followed by the counsellor being summoned to a meeting at work at the time of the next supervision. It is the responsibility of both supervisor and supervisee to see that cases are adequately covered through such periods and that telephone discussions or an alternative appointment for meeting is arranged when necessary. Colleagues, managers, those available for medical and psychiatric consultation, advisers in professional bodies and insurers are all valuable resources.

Finally, we must not lose sight of the fact that consideration of these areas is designed to bring protection to clients and often also offers counsellors security and protection for their decisions and actions. Perhaps the biggest fear is being taken to court, but we need to remember that, whilst litigation is on the increase, it is still very rare in relation to counselling where neglect of duty of care is more difficult to prove compared with most medical treatments. Whilst much remains unclear, and will continue to be so until tested by case law, the lack of case law is in itself an indication of a low level of legal activity in this area. In the current situation there will be various opinions about what is safe or good practice and it is important to be informed of these and to be aware when the tide of opinion is changing in a particular area.

Medical and psychiatric issues can also be potentially an enjoyable and rewarding part of counselling. In good work settings it can provide opportunities for positive collaboration with colleagues as well as a good outcome for clients. With increasing experience of counselling anxieties tend to diminish and concerns become less and, as a result, it is more possible to enjoy the expansion of knowledge base and extension of skills. As confidence grows the unknown can become less threatening and more interesting and even a welcome change from the routine work. Indeed, for senior professionals everyday work can be rather bland without the opportunity to work with clients who bring the challenge of complexity.

Appendix 2   Glossary

Most of the specialist medical and psychiatric terms used in this book are defined and explained in the text. Those not so defined are included below, together with others added for convenience of reference.

Bibliotherapy
The use of books to treat mild mental health problems. These may be specifically on mental health or, for example, novels with appropriate themes.

Biophysical
Relating to a physical understanding of a biological problem.

Bipolar affective disorder
A disorder of mood in which episodes of both mania and depression. It is also known as **manic-depressive illness**.

Borderline personality
A type of personality disorder difficult to describe precisely and concisely. Such people are impulsive, poor at personal relationships, unpredictable and sometimes can seem to be on the point of losing touch with reality.

Care Plan
A coherent approach to someone's mental health problems that co-ordinates the input of the professionals involved and ensures that they are appropriate and complement each other.

Chemotherapy
The treatment of illness by medication, commonly used particularly in such treatment of cancer.

Clinical governance
A process which aims to assure and improve clinical standards in service delivery.

Cognitive-Analytic Therapy (CAT)
A structured short-term treatment that combines *psychodynamic* and cognitive features.

Cognitive-behavioural therapy (CBT)
A structured psychological treatment which seeks to change problem behaviours and dysfunctional patterns of thought and beliefs. See also *systematic desensitisation*.

CORE (Clinical Outcomes in Routine Evaluation)
A set of questionnaire forms used routinely and widely in NHS settings to evaluate risk and to provide evidence of service quality and effectiveness.

Dementia
An organic disorder of the brain involving loss of intellectual ability and memory and also changes of personality. It can be caused by a number of conditions, the most common of which is Alzheimer's disease.

Appendix 1   Suggested Reading

Chapter 4   Issues in Established Counselling and in Supervision
Abel Smith, A., Irving, J. and Brown, P. (1989) Counselling in the medical context, in Dryden, W., Charles-Edwards, D. and Woolfe, R., *Handbook of Counselling in Britain*. London: Tavistock/Routledge, pp. 122–33.
Counselman, E.F. and Alonso, A. (1993) The ill therapist; therapists' reactions to personal illness and its impact on psychotherapy, *American Journal of Psychotherapy* 47(4): 591–602.

Chapter 6   Taking Account of Psychiatric Conditions and Their Treatment
Gelder, M., Gath, D. and Mayou, R. (1989) *Oxford Textbook of Psychiatry* (2nd edition). Oxford: Oxford University Press.

Chapter 7   Safety and Safeguards
BAC *Code of Ethics and Practice for Counsellors*.
BAC *Code of Ethics and Practice for the Supervision of Counsellors*.
BACP Information Sheet
 P4: *Guidance for ethical decision making: a suggested model for practitioners*. Lynne Gabriel and Roger Casemore.
Bond, T. (2000) *Standards and Ethics for Counselling in Action*. London: Sage.
Bond, T. (1993) When to protect a client from self-destruction, in Dryden W. (ed) *Questions and Answers on Counselling in Action*. London: Sage, pp. 118–23.

Diagnosis
The label given to a set of *symptoms* and *signs* based on their co-existence and confirmed with observed pathological phenomena.

Electro-convulsive therapy (ECT)
The treatment of mental disorders, particularly depression, by passing an electric current through the brain with the use of anaesthesia and a muscle relaxant.

E-therapy
E-mail correspondence with a counsellor or psychotherapist, which may be suitable for those who are reticent about face-to-face contact with a counsellor and those who do not live near a practice, or have restricted mobility.

Flashbacks
Sudden returns to earlier experiences. There can be a number of causes for this, including a history of traumatic experiences or of taking hallucinogenic drugs.

Heart arrhythmias
Variations from the normal heartbeat.

Inter-Personal Therapy (IPT)
A short-term psychological treatment focusing on social functioning and relationships.

Magnetic Resonance Imaging (MRI) scanning
A (non-invasive) investigative procedure for visualising the structure of the brain. It can also be used to reveal how the brain functions.

Mania
A state of extreme euphoria and over-activity often involving socially unacceptable behaviour.

Manic-depressive illness
A disorder of mood in which episodes of both mania and depression. Also known as *bipolar affective disorder*.

Motivational interviewing
An approach to interviewing which aims to help a person to decide whether or not they wish to change their behaviour.

Neuro-psychological
Relating to the interaction between the brain, and thoughts and behaviour.

Osteoporosis
A bone disease, especially found in women over fifty, involving loss of bone tissue.

Ovulation
The movement of a human egg towards a woman's uterus, taking place approximately half-way through the menstrual cycle.

Parkinson's disease
A progressive disease of the nervous system, usually occurring in later life, and involving tremor and progressive disability.

Parkinsonism
Symptoms similar to Parkinson's disease but following on from viral infections and some drugs.

Pathology
Change in the structure or function of the body caused by disease.

Post-traumatic stress disorder
A disorder caused by a traumatic event outside the range of usual experience, characterised by a cluster of symptoms including anxiety, *flashbacks*, nightmares and guilt.

Pre-term delivery
A delivery of a baby that occurs before the completion of the full term of pregnancy (37 weeks).

Psychodynamic
An approach that uses a dynamic understanding of the mind derived from psychoanalytic concepts such as the unconscious and psychological defences. See also *cognitive-analytic therapy*.

Psychosocial
Involving both the mind and social factors.

Schizophrenia
A group of disorders leading to mental deterioration such as distortion of thinking, delusions and a disturbed sense of self.

Secondary gain
This is where disability reaps benefits such as care and attention, a cessation of difficult responsibilities, or some resolution of personal conflicts or disappointments.

Signs
Objective physical changes, usually detected by physical examination. See also *symptoms* and *diagnosis*.

Somatic
Relating to the body.

Somatisation
The expression of psychological problems through apparently physical disease.

SSRI
Selective Serotonin Reuptake Inhibitor. Commonest type of antidepressant drug which works to increase the level of serotonin in the brain (known to be decreased in severe depression).

Stepped care
An approach to mental health problems whereby the treatment approach is adjusted according to the severity of the problem. See Figure 6.1 in Chapter 6.

Symptoms
Those words used by people to express unusual or uncomfortable phenomena, such as pain, dizziness or diarrhoea. See also *signs* and *diagnosis*.

Syndrome
A collection of *symptoms* that can be recognised as commonly occurring together in an identifiable pattern. See also *diagnosis*.

Systematic desensitisation
A behavioural treatment combining progressive exposure to a feared object or situation together with a method of controlling the person's anxiety arousal (see also *Cognitive-Behavioural Therapy*).

Thyroid
A gland near the larynx which produces hormones vital in maintaining normal growth and body functioning.

Appendix 3   Useful Organisations and Internet Addresses

British Association for Counselling and Psychotherapy
www.bacp.co.uk

British National Formulary
www.bnf.org

CORE
www.coreims.co.uk

Depression Alliance
www.depressionalliance.org

Mental Health Foundation
www.mentalhealth.org.uk

Mind
www.mind.org.uk

National Phobics Society
www.phobics-society.org.uk

NHS Direct
www.nhsdirect.nhs.uk

Royal College of Psychiatrists
www.rcpsych.ac.uk

Sane
www.sane.org.uk/public_html/index.shtml

UK Council for Psychotherapy
www.psychotherapy.org.uk

References

American Psychiatric Association (1994) *Desk Reference to the Diagnostic Criteria from DSM-IV.* New York: American Psychiatric Press.

Altschuler, J. (1997) *Working with Chronic Illness: a family approach.* Palgrave Macmillan.

BACP Ethical Framework (2002) Rugby: British Association for Counselling and Psychotherapy.

BACP Information Sheets:

> DG 9: *Clinical governance in counselling and psychotherapy in the NHS.* Michael Carter.
>
> G2: *Confidentiality: counselling and the law.* Alan Jamieson and Tim Bond.
>
> G5: *Personal safety for practitioners working in high-risk environments and with high-risk clients.* Harry Jackson (revised by Denise Chaytor).
>
> P4: *Guidance for ethical decision making: a suggested model for practitioners.* Lynne Gabriel and Roger Casemore.
>
> P7: *Working with the suicidal client.* Andrew Reeves and Pat Seber.
>
> P9: *Am I fit to practise as a counsellor?* Heather Dale.

Ball, V. (1993) *Guidelines for the Employment of Counsellors in General Practice.* Rugby: Counselling in Medical Settings/BAC.

Bancroft, J. (1989) *Human Sexuality and Its Problems* (2nd edn). Edinburgh: Churchill Livingstone.

Bayliss, J. (2004) *Counselling Skills in Palliative Care.* Salisbury: Key Books.

Berke, J.H. (1979) *I Haven't Had to go Mad Here: The Psychotic's Journey from Dependence to Autonomy.* London: Pelican.

Bird, L. (1999) *The Fundamental Facts: All The Latest Facts and Figures on Mental Illness.* London: Mental Health Foundation.

Blake, F., Salkovskis, P., Gath, D., Day, A. and Garrod, A. (1998) Cognitive therapy for premenstrual syndrome: a controlled trial, *Journal of Psychosomatic Research* 45: 307–18.

Bond, T. (1993) When to protect a client from self-destruction, in Dryden, W. (ed.) *Questions and Answers on Counselling in Action.* London: Sage, pp. 118–23.

Bond, T. (2000) *Standards and Ethics for Counselling in Action* (2nd edn). London: Sage.

Bower, P. (2002) Primary care mental health workers: models of working and evidence of effectiveness, *British Journal of General Practice* 52: 926–33.

Bower, P., Rowland, N. and Hardy, R. (2003) The clinical effectiveness of counselling in primary care: a systematic review and meta-analysis. *Psychological Medicine* 33: 203–15.

British Association for Counselling and Psychotherapy (2002) *Ethical Framework for Good Practice in Counselling and Psychotherapy.* Rugby: BACP.

Broome, A.K. (ed.) (1989) *Health Psychology*. London: Chapman & Hall.

Browne, F. (2000) Commentary, *Advances in Psychiatric Treatment* 6: 411–13.

Burton, M. and Watson, M. (1988) *Counselling People with Cancer*. Chichester: Wiley.

Clare, A. (2001) *Psychiatry in Dissent: Controversial Issues in Thought and Practice* (Reprinted). London: Routledge.

Clinical Standards Advisory Group (1994) *Back Pain*. London: Her Majesty's Stationery Office.

Cohen, K. (1992) Some legal issues in counselling and psychotherapy, *British Journal of Guidance and Counselling* 20: 10–26.

Colombo, A., Bendelow, G., Fulford, B. and Williams, S. (2003) Evaluating the influence of implicit models of mental disorder on processes of shared decision making within community-based multi-disciplinary teams, *Social Science and Medicine* 56: 1557–70.

Cooper, C.W. (1993) Vestibular neuronitis: a review of a common cause of vertigo in general practice, *British Journal of General Practice* 43: 164–7.

Cooper, I.S. (1973) *The Victim is Always the Same*. New York: Harper & Row.

Cope, H., David, A., Pelosi, A. and Mann, A. (1994) Predictors of chronic post viral fatigue, *Lancet* 344: 864–8.

CORE System Group (1998) *Clinical Outcomes in Routine Evaluation System*. Leeds: The Psychological Therapies Research Centre.

Counselman, E.F. and Alonso, A. (1993) The ill therapist; therapists' reactions to personal illness and its impact on psychotherapy, *American Journal of Psychotherapy* 47: 591–602.

Daly, R.J. (1993) Suicide in depressed patients, *British Journal of Psychiatry* 163 (suppl. 20): 29–32.

Davidson, R., Rollnick, S. and MacEwan, I. (1991) *Counselling Problem Drinkers*. London: Routledge.

Davis, J. and Chipman, M. (1997) Stalkers and other obsessional types: A review and forensic psychological typology of those who stalk, *Journal of Clinical Forensic Medicine* 4: 166–73.

Davis, J., Siota, R.L. and Stewart, L.M. (1999) Future prediction of dangerousness and violent behavior: psychological indicators and considerations for conducting an assessment of potential threat, *Canadian Journal of Clinical Medicine* 6: 44–58.

Davy, J. and Ellis, S. (2000) *Counselling Skills in Palliative Care*. Buckingham: Open University Press.

Department of Health (1997) *The New NHS: Modern, Dependable*. London: Department of Health.

Department of Health (2001) *Treatment Choice in Psychological Therapies and Counselling Evidence Based Clinical Practice Guidelines*. London: Department of Health.

Department of Health (2002) *The National Service Framework for Mental Health: modern standards and service models*. London: Department of Health.

Department of Health (2005) *Raising the Standard: The revised National Service Framework for adult mental health services in Wales*. London: Department of Health.

Dickson, A. and Henriques, N. (1992) *Menopause. The Woman's View*. London: Quartet Books.

Doll, H., Brown, S., Thurston, A. and Vessey, Y.M. (1989) Pyridoxine (vitamin B6) and the premenstrual syndrome: a randomised cross-over trial, *Journal of the Royal College of General Practitioners* 39: 364–8.

Dryden, W. and Neenhan, M. (2004) *Counselling Individuals: a rational emotive behavioural handbook* (4th edn). London: Whurr Publications.

Eldrid, J. (1988) *Caring for the Suicidal.* London: Constable.

Eysenck, H. (1992) The outcome problem in psychotherapy, in Dryden, W. and Feltham, C. (eds) *Psychotherapy and its Discontents.* Buckingham: Open University Press, pp. 100–34.

Fairburn, C.G. and Harrison, P.J. (2003) Eating disorders, *Lancet* 361(9355): 407–16.

Farthing, M.J.G. (1995) Irritable bowel, irritable body or irritable brain? *British Medical Journal* 310: 171–5.

Feinsilver, D.B. (1998) The therapist as a person facing death: the hardest of external realities and therapeutic action, *International Journal of Psychoanalysis* 79: 131–50.

Fernando, S. (2003) *Cultural Diversity, Mental Health and Society: the struggle against racism.* London: Brunner-Routledge.

Fisher, M. (1996) How do members of an interprofessional clinical team adjust to hospice care? *Palliative Medicine* 10: 319–28.

Fox, R. and Cooper, M. (1998) Effects of suicide on the private therapist: a professional and personal perspective, *Clinical Social Work Journal* 26: 143–57.

France, R. and Robson, M. (1997) *Behaviour Therapy in Primary Care: a practical guide.* London: Jessica Kingsley.

Frank, D. and Mooney, B. (2002) *Hypnosis and Counselling in the Treatment of Chronic Illness.* Carmarthen: Crown House.

Friedman, G. (1991) Treatment of the irritable bowel syndrome, *Gastroenterology Clinics of North America* 20: 325–33.

Freeth, R. (2001) Ending therapy ... when one's therapist dies, *Counselling and Psychotherapy Journal* 12: 18–20.

Gardner, W.N. and Bass, C. (1989) Hyperventilation in clinical practice, *British Journal of Hospital Medicine* 41: 73–81.

Gask, L. (1995) Management in primary care, in *Treatment of Functional Somatic Symptoms* (eds) Mayou, R., Bass, C. and Sharpe, M. Oxford: OUP.

Gask, L., Morris, R. and Goldberg, D. (2002) *Reattribution: managing patients who somatise emotional distress.* Manchester University Department of Psychiatry (2nd edn) 1999.

Goldberg, L., Gask, L. and O'Dowd, T. (1989) The treatment of somatisation: teaching the techniques of reattribution. *Journal of Psychosomatic Research* 33: 689–95.

Grol, R. (ed.) (1981) *To Heal or to Harm. The Prevention of Somatic Fixation in General Practice.* London: Royal College of General Practitioners.

Guthrie, E., Creed, F.M. and Dawson, D. (1993) Controlled study of psychotherapy in irritable bowel syndrome, *British Journal of Psychiatry* 163: 315–21.

Hammersley, D. (1995) *Counselling People on Prescribed Drugs.* London: Sage.

Haynes, J. (1996) Death of the analyst: the end is where we start from, *Harvest* 42(1): 27–44.

Haynes, R.B., Sackett, D.L., Taylor, D.E., Gibson, E.S. and Johnson, A.L. (1978) Increased absenteeism from work after detection and labelling of hypertensive patients, *New England Journal of Medicine* 299: 741–4.

Higgs, R. and Dammers, J. (1992) Ethical issues in counselling and primary care, *British Journal of Guidance and Counselling* 20: 27–38.

Holmes, G.P., Kaplan, J.E., Gantz, N.M., Komaroff, A.L., Schonberger, L.B., Straus, S.E., Jones, J.F., Dubois, R.E., Cunningham-Rundles, C., Pahwa, S., Tosato, G., Zagans, L.S., Purtilo, D.T., Brown, N., Schooley, R.T. and Brus, I. (1988) Chronic fatigue a working definition, *Annals of Internal Medicine* 108: 387–9.

Ho-Yen Do (1990) Patient management of post-viral fatigue syndrome, *British Journal of General Practice* 40: 37–9.

Humphrey, M. (1989) *Back Pain.* London: Tavistock/Routledge.

Hunter, M. (1994) *Counselling in Obstetrics and Gynaecology.* Leicester: BPS Books.

James, W. (1977) *The Varieties of Religious Experience: A study in human nature.* Glasgow: Collins.

Jayson, M.I.V. (1994) Mechanisms underlying chronic back pain, *British Medical Journal* 309: 681–2.

Jeffries, R. (2000) The disappearing counsellor, *Counselling,* September: 478–81.

Jenkins, P. (1992) Counselling and the law, *Counselling,* August: 165–7.

Jenkins, P. (1997) *Counselling, Psychotherapy and the Law.* London: Sage.

Jenkins, P., Kerr, V. and Stone, J. (2004) *Psychotherapy and the Law.* London, Whurr.

Johnson, C. and Webster, D. (2002) *Recrafting a Life: coping with chronic illness and pain.* New York: Brunner-Routledge.

Kamphuis, J.H. and Emmelkamp, P.M. (2000) Stalking – a contemporary challenge for forensic and clinical psychiatry, *British Journal of Psychiatry,* 176: 206–9.

Kelleher, D. (1988) *Diabetes.* London: Tavistock/Routledge.

Kendell, R.E. (1975) *The Role of Diagnosis in Psychiatry.* Oxford: Blackwell.

Kennedy, I. (1988) *Treat Me Right: essays in medical law and ethics.* Oxford: Clarendon Press.

Kennedy, I. and Grubb, A. (1994) *Medical Law.* London: Butterworth.

Kettell, J., Jones, R. and Lydeard, S. (1992) Reasons for consultation in irritable bowel syndrome: symptoms and patient characteristics, *British Journal of General Practice* 42: 459–61.

Laing, R.D. and Esterson, A. (1970) *Sanity, Madness and the Family.* Harmondsworth: Penguin.

Lair, G.S. (1996) *Counselling the Terminally Ill. Sharing the Journey.* London: Taylor & Francis.

Lambert, M.J. and Ogles, B.M. (2003) The efficacy and effectiveness of psychotherapy, in *Handbook of Psychotherapy and Behavior Change* (5th edn) (eds) Bergin, A.E., Garfield, S.L. and Lambert, M.J. New York: John Wiley.

Lawrie, S.M. and Pelosi, A.J. (1994) Chronic fatigue syndrome: prevalence and outcome, *British Medical Journal* 308: 732–3.

Lazarus, A.A. (1989) *The Practice of Multimodal Therapy.* Baltimore: Johns Hopkins University Press.

Levy, S.M. (1990) Humanizing death: psychotherapy with terminally ill patients, in Herek, G.M. *et al.* (ed.) *Psychological Aspects of Serious Illness: Chronic Conditions, Fatal Diseases and Clinical Care.* Washington: American Psychological Association, pp. 185–213.

MacLeod, S. (1981) *The Art of Starvation: an adolescence observed.* London: Virago.

Martin, P. (2001) The therapist as a person, *Counselling and Psychotherapy* 12: 10–13.

Mason, J.K. and McCall Smith, R.A. (1994) *Law and Medical Ethics.* London: Butterworth.

McCarty, T., Schneider-Braus, K. and Goodwin, J. (1986) Use of alternate therapist during pregnancy leave, *Journal of the American Academy of Psychoanalysis* 14: 377–83.

McClean, S. (1995) *Medical Law.* Aldershot: Dartmouth.

McMahon, G. (2000) Holiday cover, *Counselling* 11: 298–9.

McMahon, G. and Lewis, J. (2001a) Are you sitting comfortably? *Counselling and Psychotherapy Journal* 12: 34–5.

McMahon, G. and Lewis, J. (2001b) Posture at work, *Counselling and Psychotherapy Journal* 12: 40–1.

Meloy, J.R. (2000) *Violence Risk and Threat Assessment: a practical guide for mental health and criminal justice professionals.* Specialized Training Services, San Diego, CA.

Meloy, J.R., Davis, B. and Lovette, J. (2001) Risk factors for violence among stalkers, *Journal of Threat Assessment* 1: 13–16.

Miller, W.R. and Rollnick, S. (1992) *Motivational Interviewing: preparing people to change addictive behaviour*. Guildford Press.

Monks, P. and Martin, L. (1997) A deaf counsellor: can it work? *Counselling* 8: 263–5.

Morgan, D. (1999) *Stalking*. IAFP Newsletter 3 at www.psyctc.org/iafp/nl_3_1/stalking.html

Mullen, P., Pathe, M. and Purcell, R. (2000) *Stalkers and their Victims*. Cambridge University Press.

Mynors-Wallis, L. (2005) *Problem-Solving Treatment for Anxiety and Depression. A Practical Guide*. Oxford: Oxford University Press.

NICE (2002) Schizophrenia: Full national clinical guidelines on core interventions in primary and secondary care. www.nice.org.uk/pdf/cg001fullguideline.pdf

NICE (2004a) Core interventions in the treatment and management of anorexia nervosa, bulimia nervosa and related eating disorders. CG 009 Eating disorders. www.nice.org.uk/pdf/cg009niceguidance.pdf

NICE (2004b) Management of anxiety (panic disorder, with or without agoraphobia, and generalised anxiety disorder) in adults in primary, secondary and community care. CG22 Anxiety www.nice.org.uk/pdf/CG022NICEguideline.pdf

NICE (2004c) Management of depression in primary and secondary care. CG 23 Depression www.nice.org.uk/pdf/CG023NICEguideline.pdf

NICE (2005) Obsessive-compulsive disorder: core interventions in the treatment of obsessive-compulsive disorder and body dysmorphic disorder CG 31 Obsessive-compulsive disorder www.nice.org.uk/pdf/cg031niceguideline.pdf

Nicolson, P. (1992) The construction of female psychology, in *Cognition and the Menstrual Cycle*, ed. Richardson, J.T.E. New York: Springer-Verlag.

Orbach, S. (2006) *Fat is a Feminist Issue*. London: Arrow.

Palmer, R.L. (2000) *Helping People with Eating Disorders: a clinical guide to assessment and treatment*. Chichester: John Wiley.

Palmer, S. and Dryden, W. (1995) *Counselling for Stress Problems*. London: Sage.

Passmore, H.S. (1973) The patient's use of his doctor, in *Six Minutes for the Patient*, (eds) Balint, E. and Norell, J.S. London: Tavistock.

Pearce, S. and Wardle, J. (eds) (1989) *The Practice of Behavioural Medicine*. Oxford: BPS Books.

Pendleton, D., Schofield, T., Tate, P. and Havelock, P. (1984) *The Consultation. An Approach to Learning and Teaching*. Oxford: Oxford University Press.

Pfeffer, J.M. and Waldron, G. (1987*) Psychiatric Differential Diagnosis*. Edinburgh: Churchill Livingstone.

Pollin, I.P. (1995) *Medical Crisis Counselling*. New York: Norton.

Quinn, N. (1995) Parkinsonism–recognition and differential diagnosis, *British Medical Journal* 310: 447–52.

Rack, P. (1982) *Race, Culture and Mental Disorder*. London: Tavistock.

Read, N. (2005) *Sick and Tired – Healing the Illnesses Doctors Cannot Cure*. London: Weidenfeld & Nicolson.

Rassool, G.H. (1998) *Substance Use and Misuse*. Oxford: Blackwell.

Reeves, A. and Mintz, R. (2001) The experience of therapists who work with suicidal clients: an exploratory study, *Counselling and Psychotherapy Research Journal* 2: 37–42.

Richards, J.P. (1990) Postnatal depression: a review of recent literature, *British Journal of General Practice* 40: 472–6.

Richards, B.M. (2000) Impact upon therapy and the therapist when working with suicidal patients: some transference and countertransference aspects, *British Journal of Guidance and Counselling* 28: 325–37.

Richardson, J.T.E. (1989) Student learning and the menstrual cycle: premenstrual symptoms and approaches to studying, *Educational Psychology*: 215–38.

Ridsdale, L., Evans, A. and Jerrett, W. (1993) Patients with fatigue in general practice: a prospective study, *British Medical Journal* 307: 103–6.

Robinson, I. (1988) *Multiple Sclerosis.* London: Tavistock/Routledge.

Romans, J., Hays, J. and White, T. (1996) Stalking and related behaviors experienced by counseling center staff members from current or former clients, *Professional Psychology: Research and Practice* 27: 595–9.

Rose, C. (2004) Needing a break, *Counselling and Psychotherapy Journal* 15(7): 26–8.

Rose, S., Bisson, J. and Wessely, S. (2003) A systematic review of single-session psychological interventions ('debriefing') following trauma, *Psychotherapy and Psychosomatics* 72: 176–84.

Rosenfield, M. (1997) *Counselling by Telephone.* London: Sage.

Royal College of Physicians (2003) *The Psychological Care of Medical Patients.* A practical guide. Chapter 2, Communication and psychological assessment. Report of joint working party of the Royal College of Physicians and the Royal College of Psychiatrists (2nd edn).

Rudd, M.D., Jobes, D.A., Joiner, T.E. and King, C.A. (1999) The outpatient treatment of suicidality: An integration of science and recognition of its limitations, *Professional Psychology – Research and Practice* 30: 437–46.

Ryle, A. (1997) *Cognitive Analytic Therapy and Borderline Personality Disorder: The Model and the Method.* Chichester: John Wiley.

Sacks, O. (1986) *The Man Who Mistook His Wife For a Hat.* London: Pan.

Sandberg, D.A. McNiel, D.E. and Binder, R.L. (1998) Characteristics of psychiatric inpatients who stalk, threaten, or harass hospital staff after discharge, *American Journal of Psychiatry* 155: 1102–5.

Scambler, G. (1989) *Epilepsy.* London: Tavistock/Routledge.

Schaverien, J. (2002) *The Dying Patient in Psychotherapy Desire, Dreams and Individuation.* Basingstoke: Palgrave Macmillan.

Scott, M.J. and Stradling, S.G. (2000) *Counselling for Post-Traumatic Stress Disorder.* London: Sage.

Sharpe, M., Hawton, K., Simkin, S., Surawy, C., Hackmann, A., Klimes, I., O Peto, T., Warrell, D. and Seagroatt, V. (1996) Cognitive behaviour therapy for the chronic fatigue syndrome: a randomised controlled trial, *British Medical Journal* 312: 22–6.

Sibbald, B., White, P., Pharoah, C., Freeling, P. and Anderson, H.R. (1988) Relationship between psychological factors and asthma morbidity, *Family Practice* 5: 12–17.

Sibbald, B. Addington-Hall, J., Brenneman, D. *et al.* (1993) Counsellors in English and Welsh general practices: their nature and distribution, *British Medical Journal* 306: 29–33.

Silverman, J.D., Kurtz, S.M. and Draper, J. (1998) *Skills for Communicating with Patients.* Oxford: Radcliffe Medical Press.

Sims, A. (2003) *Symptoms in the Mind: An introduction to descriptive pathology* (3rd edn). Edinburgh: Saunders.

Striano, J. (1988) *Can Psychotherapists Hurt You?* Santa Barbara: Professional Press.

Styron, W. (1992) *Darkness Visible.* London: Picador.

Sutherland, S. (1987) *Breakdown: a personal crisis and a medical dilemma.* Oxford: Oxford University Press.

Taylor, S.E. and Aspinwall, L.G. (1990) Psychosocial aspects of chronic illness, in Herek, G.M. *et al.* (ed.) *Psychological Aspects of Serious Illness: Chronic Conditions, Fatal Diseases and Clinical Care.* Washington: American Psychological Association, pp. 3–60.

Thompson, M., Rose, C., Wainright, W., Mattar, L. and Scanlan, M. (2001) Activities of counsellors on a hospice/palliative care environment, *Journal of Palliative Care* 17: 229–328.

Trayner, B. and Clarkson, P. (1992) What happens if a psychotherapist dies? *Counselling* 3: 23–4.

Tuckett, D., Boulton, M., Olson, C. and Williams, A. (1985) *Meetings Between Experts.* London: Tavistock.

Usherwood, T. (1987) Factors affecting estimates of the prevalence of asthma and wheezing in childhood, *Family Practice* 4: 318–21.

Usherwood, T.P. (1990) Responses to illness – implications for the clinician, *Journal of the Royal Society of Medicine* 83: 205–7.

Waddell, G. (1993) Simple low back pain: rest or active exercise? *Annals of Rheumatic Disease* 52: 317–19.

Walker, M. (1990) *Women in Therapy and Counselling.* Milton Keynes: Open University Press.

Walton, J.N. (1989) *Essentials of Neurology.* London: Pitman.

Wearden, A.J., Morriss, R.K., Mullis, R. *et al.* (1998) Randomised, double-blind, placebo-controlled treatment trial of fluoxetine and graded exercise for chronic fatigue syndrome, *British Journal of Psychiatry* 172: 485–90.

Wessely, S., Chalder, T., Hirsch, S. *et al.* (1995) Postinfectious fatigue: prospective cohort in primary care, *Lancet* 345: 1333–8.

WHO staff (1993) *The ICD-10 Classification of Mental and Behavioural Diseases.* Geneva: WHO see www.who.int/classifications/icd/en/ for on-line version and www.mentalneurologicalprimarycare.org for primary care version adapted for the UK.

Worden, J.W. (2003) *Grief Counselling and Grief Therapy: a handbook for the mental health practitioner.* London: Brunner-Routledge.

Index